Discovering Your

Amazing Marriage

Understanding the Power of Choice

Learn How to Communicate Effectively

How to Protect Your Marriage From Infidelity

Discovering Your
Amazing
Marriage

Understanding the Power of Choice

Learn How to Communicate Effectively

How to Protect Your Marriage From Infidelity

JASON & DEBBY COLEMAN

SERAPHINA
PRESS

SERAPHINA PRESS

212 3RD AVENUE NORTH, SUITE 290

MINNEAPOLIS, MN 55401

612.455.2293

WWW.SERAPHINAPRESS.COM

ISBN - 978-0-9841965-3-1

ISBN - 0-9841965-3-6

LCCN - 2010926519

COVER DESIGN AND TYPESET BY JAMES ARNESON

PRINTED IN THE UNITED STATES OF AMERICA

Contents

This book is dedicated, first and foremost, to our children, Jessalyn, Ariana, Abigale, and Hunter. We trust and pray that through the choices we have made, both good and bad, you will learn to make wise and prudent decisions, and, ultimately, discover an amazing marriage yourself. Secondly, to our friends who have loved us and supported us through the process of writing this book; particularly those of you who have been asking, "How's the book going?" for months on end and keeping us motivated. We love you all and it is our desire that you, too, discover the amazing marriage we know you are capable of achieving. Thanks for the encouragement and support!

Paper or plastic? Chicken or fish? Latte or cappuccino? "Skinny" or whole milk? Public school or private? PS2, X-Box, or Wii? Made in China or Made in the U.S.A.? We are bombarded with literally hundreds of choices every day! We are blessed in many ways to live in America, where we have freedom of choice. But have you ever considered the concept of *too many* choices? What's a person to do? You can't even order coffee anymore without having to make multiple decisions.

Do you ever find yourself wishing some things in life were less confusing or complicated? Perhaps if you were required to make fewer choices, you would, in some regard, make better choices. Perhaps you would focus on how these choices would impact you for the long term, rather than just the here and now. Then again, there may be times you long for more choices. Times when the options available to you don't fit your requirements, your mood, your budget, or what you would call an ideal situation. The bottom line is that the choices we all make impact our lives in ways we may not even realize.

If you are married, one of the most important decisions or choices you have made in life is with whom to spend your life. The *rest* of your life. As you read through the chapters of this book, it is our desire that you look at your marriage with a new perspective and that you understand that you didn't "fall in love" with your spouse, you *chose to love* your spouse.

You will see that love is a choice, and that every day you can choose to make your marriage what you want it to be. It is your life. It is your choice how you spend it and with whom you spend it. The choices you make ultimately determine the quality of your life and the quality of your marriage. Wrong choices can be so costly; right choices can be so rewarding. Choose wisely.

Several months ago, as we were talking one night, we realized that no less than five different couples that are friends of ours asked us to intervene in their marriage within a period of four weeks. Paul asked me for advice on how to handle an issue with his wife. Mark asked me to pray for him and his wife, as they were expecting their first child but they were not communicating with one another, and it was driving a wedge between them. Jonathan admitted to having an inappropriate relationship with another woman, and wanted nothing more than to seek forgiveness and restoration with his wife. Amy broke down and cried while having coffee with Debby one day, and unloaded the pent-up pain and misery she felt because of her failing marriage. In an e-mail, Cathy told Debby of some serious health problems her daughter was fighting and asked her for advice on how she and her husband could work through this without blaming one other.

Debby and I have been married for over twenty years and have made more mistakes than we care to remember, much less write about. Through the years, we have seen so many of our friends locked in marriages that are, at best, mediocre. We have felt the need to write this book for over three years now, and have come to the conclusion that time is running out on so many people we care for and love. We may not have all the answers, but we trust you will be able to identify with some of what we have to say, and it is our desire that we help you achieve the amazing marriage that you and your spouse deserve.

We began our life together on September 30, 1989, after dating for two years. On our wedding day, someone close to Debby told her that she didn't think we would last three years together. Wow, imagine hearing that on your wedding day! We were both young, but we had been engaged for over a year, and that comment came as a surprise to Debby. We both look back and agree that our first year together was the worst year of our lives, but we are glad to confirm that we made it beyond the three-year expectancy and are still going strong!

During our first year of marriage, our perfect little world was rocked and our marriage was tested as no marriage should be tested. Our separate lives had been thrust together suddenly and we were both so very young and immature, thinking we would have a Cinderella fairy-tale story. Nothing could have been further from the truth. The reality of coming together as husband and wife at such a young age challenged both of us immediately upon saying "I do." Neither of us was ready, let alone prepared, for what being married meant as far as sacrifice and change of lifestyle. I imagine many, if not most, couples experience similar challenges.

Within the first six months of our marriage, we had to deal with the consequences of infidelity and the very real possibility of divorce. What happened to our relationship in such a short period of time? These things aren't supposed to happen at all; but if they do, it's usually later in life when married people drift away from each other. Or so we thought. We now know through our own experiences that nothing can destroy a marriage quicker than infidelity, but we also know that we have a story to tell that may encourage couples to stay the course and make their marriage work, no matter what challenges they may face. We are a living testimony of the power of forgiveness and restoration.

In the midst of dealing with the infidelity and the many choices we had to make, I ended up in the emergency room with a collapsed lung. Debby was faced with the very real possibility of being a widow at the young age of 19. I recovered quickly after a routine surgery, but for the next several years we struggled emotionally, financially, spiritually, and in every other way imaginable. Besides the grace of God, there was one thing that held us together through it all. That one thing is the commitment we have made to one another. We both come from divorced homes so we made it a priority and commitment from the very beginning of our married life to break that cycle of divorce.

Remarkably, we not only made it through those early years, but we have managed to build what we like to describe as an "amazing marriage." We're not perfect, and, yes, we still fight. But we understand one another and have enough love and respect for one another so that we can disagree on issues without endangering our relationship. We're not insecure in our relationship and we know that we can and will survive whatever life throws our way. We make a choice every day to make it through whatever crisis we happen to be facing on that particular day, and we choose to stay the course.

Our desire is to write a book that empowers people to unlock their potential to develop and maintain an amazing marriage. In the following pages, you will find practical tools and suggestions for strengthening your relationship and growing closer to your partner, if you apply the principles herein to your marriage.

We attribute much of our happiness and commitment to each other to our sacred religious vows and our relationship with God, though we acknowledge that not everyone shares those same beliefs. At the end of each chapter, you will find a biblical perspective on the principles reviewed. This perspective helps explain the principles from a Christian perspective. You may choose not to read the biblical perspective; that's up to you. That is one of the many choices you get to make in life. If that perspective doesn't appeal to you, simply skip that part and go on to the

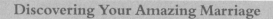

next chapter. You can certainly experience what we call an "amazing marriage" without sharing our religious beliefs.

Whether you read the biblical sections or not, we trust this book will resonate with you and help you to build bridges toward a successful marriage. We also understand that you may have a different name for God, depending on your faith—for example, Yahweh, Yeshua, Adonai, or Creator—but due to our faith, and for simplicity, we will use the name God throughout the book. We believe in the God of the Christian Bible, and His son, Jesus Christ.

Grab a cup of coffee, or your favorite beverage, and get comfortable as you begin the journey. Oh, one last thing. We want to apologize up front if we step on your toes or discuss some things that make you wince or that will strike a nerve and make you feel uncomfortable. Chances are, we will. That's where we suggest you take out your highlighter or pen and mark up your book for future reference. After all, that topic may be the very thing standing in between you and an amazing marriage.

Let's begin the journey together.

Chapter 1

Love is a Choice

"There are two primary choices in life: to accept conditions as they exist, or accept the responsibility for changing them." ~ Dr. Denis Waitley

D o you know anyone who has a truly amazing marriage? Would you categorize your marriage as "amazing," and what exactly is an amazing marriage anyhow? Have you ever thought that any marriage could actually be *amazing*? As we begin this journey together, we encourage you to unlock and discover the amazing potential within your own marriage.

For some, you have an amazing marriage already and you may just be curious to read our perspective, and perhaps take note of a few tips to further strengthen the bonds of your relationship. For others, you may have been so influenced with the Hollywood version of marriage or have been "trapped" in a mediocre marriage for so many years that you don't think an amazing marriage is possible, under any conditions.

Let's begin with an easy question. Why do people settle for "less than amazing?" We would like to suggest a simple answer: Because an amazing marriage takes work. You cannot sit back and just watch it happen. It doesn't evolve over time with little or no effort. It doesn't just happen on its own. An amazing marriage can't be purchased, won, or inherited, and it can't be found on the Internet.

An amazing marriage is the result of the choices you make each and every day. Choices about how you will treat your spouse, the level of respect you will render to your spouse, how you will talk to your spouse, and so much more. You can choose to make your marriage amazing, or you can choose to accept the status quo.

If you want your marriage to be truly dynamic and unique, you need to be purposeful about the choices you make and exercise a determined effort in building your relationship. This can't be a once-in-a-while effort, or a whenever-you-feel-like-it effort, but a consistent and daily effort. You will need to make good choices that demonstrate your commitment to your spouse.

It takes a consistent effort on a daily basis to show your mate that he or she is the most important person in your life. The choices you make will demonstrate your allegiance to your spouse and your marriage. If you are not purposeful and consistent, the best you will achieve in your relationship may be mediocrity. The choice is yours.

An amazing marriage takes daily effort and requires a significant amount of time. It requires a process that grows and evolves over time as you work at it; there is no quick-fix solution you can apply when you feel it is warranted or needed. There may be times when emotions run wild—this is when people say stupid and thoughtless things—and then to avoid a fight or confrontation, a quick-fix solution to minimize the damage may seem like the best choice.

When you apply this approach, you may improve the moment but not the relationship. Repeated quick-fix solutions may have the opposite affect; by hiding and covering up your core challenges again and again, it may be difficult to gain the trust of your spouse when a genuine effort is made. Unfortunately, these Band-Aid approaches usually do more harm than good. Oftentimes, a gift may be given in an effort to defuse a conflict or a problem. Not necessarily a bad idea or approach, as long as you realize that some things just can't be fixed with a gift, or even with an apology.

Let's define what an amazing marriage is not. It is not a perfect marriage. It is not a marriage without heartaches and hardships. It is not a marriage without disappointment and pain. It's certainly not a storybook fairy tale that ends with, "and they lived happily ever after." Unfortunately, an amazing marriage is not the norm in society, either.

We have discovered that an amazing marriage is a rare bond between a husband and a wife wherein each one knows that they are *the most important person* in the eyes of their spouse. It is special and it is unique. We know that this special bond can be realized through a consistent effort and with a daily commitment of putting the other person first, at all times.

Whether you have been married for a year, a decade, or over half a century like my grandparents (sixty years and going strong!), we believe that a marriage of excellence is possible for you. Not only is it possible, it is a worthwhile goal that will benefit you and your family over and over again, in more ways than we can list in the pages of this book. A strong and thriving marriage not only affects you, but it impacts those around you. To some degree, it is a legacy that you leave for others to emulate.

We have discovered that an amazing marriage is a rare bond between a husband and a wife wherein each one knows that they are *the most important person* in the eyes of their spouse.

An amazing marriage can be achieved, regardless of many of the circumstances you may find yourself in. It does not depend on demographics or a certain economic situation. It's not available only to those of a certain religious persuasion. It doesn't matter whether you are rich, poor, or of median income; white, black, or somewhere in-between; employed or retired . . . it is available for all who desire it and all who work toward it.

Once you have experienced the type of marriage we are defining, you will see that it is a worthwhile endeavor. You will come to appreciate it for what it is, and you will also find that it is a rare thing! You will cultivate it, and cherish it. You will realize the many benefits and strive to maintain it. You will want to experience the amazing marriage over and over again, on a daily basis.

The Evaluation Process

The first step to improve your marriage is to evaluate your current situation. Before you can make a decision on how to get where you want to go, you need to determine where you are. You need to triage your relationship and identify your strengths and weaknesses.

Have you ever been lost? Whether you took a wrong turn in a strange city or the wrong fork on the dusty trail while hiking, in order to find your way to safety or your destination you must first have a good idea where you are. You could be miles away from your intended destination or within a few hundred yards, but if you are on unfamiliar ground and you don't recognize any landmarks you may not be able to navigate yourself to where you need to be. It's no different in determining where you are in your relationship.

To accomplish this first step, set aside some time to talk with your spouse about your relationship and discuss your goals. What are your goals in terms of your family and your career? If your marriage is just

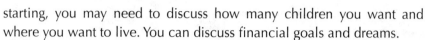

starting, you may need to discuss how many children you want and where you want to live. You can discuss financial goals and dreams.

Do you know what your spouse's goals are? Does he or she know what your goals are? Have you ever shared and discussed them together? How tragic it would be if you have committed your life to someone but you have no idea what path you are both on and where your spouse desires to go in life. Take time to openly and honestly evaluate your relationship, both as it is now and as you would like it to be. Find out what goals your spouse has for your marriage. It is important to identify goals that you both have in common and make this an integral part of your discussion.

Write out your short term (one to five years) and long term (ten plus years) goals, and then discuss them together. You may want to write them out over the course of a few days so you have time to really think them through, and then come together at an appointed time to discuss them. These goals should include the goals you have a realistic shot at achieving, as well as those hard to reach goals. Include your dreams, hopes, desires, and wishes.

After reading your spouse's goals, are you surprised? Are there goals written down that you had no idea were important to your spouse? Did you learn something about your husband or wife based on their goals? If so, this information can be important in improving the quality of your relationship. Hopefully there are goals that you both have in common that you can build upon.

Spend some time discussing each goal and allow your partner time to express their thoughts regarding those goals. Most likely, this will take more time than you will anticipate. Don't rush through this step. It may be wise to initially discuss the goals and then re-visit them a few days later, after giving them some additional thought.

Make sure that your discussions about these short- and long term goals are clear and specific. After some discussion you may want to re-vise or re-write some of the goals. Avoid setting goals that are vague, too general, or hard to measure. Goals should be achievable, but not without some effort; and they should be something that you can monitor and measure. Your goals should be specific and as detailed as possible. If needed, provide clarity so you both understand what the criteria is for achieving your goals.

Once you identify individual and shared goals, move to the next question: What will it take to achieve the needs and desires of your spouse?

How can you help your spouse achieve his or her individual goals, and what will it take for your shared goals to be reached? Basically, what you are trying to find out is, What would an amazing marriage look like to you and your spouse?

As you are identifying and discussing your goals, write out a few descriptive words that would describe your relationship. Don't describe your relationship as you want it to be, but as it currently is. It is important that you are honest and transparent with yourself and with each other. You may describe your relationship as fulfilling, adventurous, fresh, and exciting; or, perhaps your relationship would better be described as combative, empty, and unfulfilling. Understanding this is an important part of developing a plan to improve your relationship.

With this information in hand, write a plan of action that will enable you to accomplish the goals you have both agreed upon. This plan needs to include steps you can take immediately, as well as progressive steps you will initiate when you achieve certain checkpoints you establish. This plan of action should not be rigid, but should have flexibility built in. As time goes by and your circumstances change, you will need to adjust the plan to fit your current situation. As a sailor adjusts his sails to the differing wind conditions, you also need to re-evaluate and adjust your plan as your circumstances change. Write this plan down and keep it in a visible location which will be a reminder for you to stay the course to accomplish and fulfill those goals.

During this discussion, if you discover there are challenges that need to be overcome in your relationship, don't throw your spouse under the bus or belittle your spouse for shortcomings and failures. Be honest with yourself and with each other. Explain to your spouse, as clearly as possible, how you feel about your relationship. Let him or her know how you perceive your relationship and what you would like to see changed. Include the things that are most important to you, as well as those things that cause you pain.

Failing to address specific concerns will prevent you from achieving your goal of cultivating an amazing marriage. Problems left unaddressed will come back to haunt you later, and may be even more difficult if not addressed. One of my mentors for many years, Jay Cruze, likes to say, "What is uncomfortable to say now, pales in comparison to what is needed to be said when you need to readdress the problem."

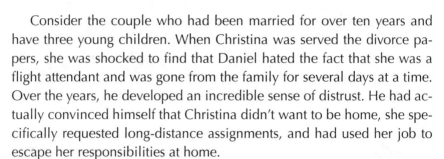

Consider the couple who had been married for over ten years and have three young children. When Christina was served the divorce papers, she was shocked to find that Daniel hated the fact that she was a flight attendant and was gone from the family for several days at a time. Over the years, he developed an incredible sense of distrust. He had actually convinced himself that Christina didn't want to be home, she specifically requested long-distance assignments, and had used her job to escape her responsibilities at home.

Furthermore, the divorce papers accused Christina of extra-marital affairs during these trips. There was no evidence or suggestion of an affair, but Daniel's distrust of her was allowed to grow and blossom over time and he had eventually convinced himself that she was unfaithful. This led Daniel to fear the worst; he began to trust her less and less, and distanced himself from her in most areas of their life.

Little did Christina know that Daniel felt this way toward her career, because he never expressed his true feelings and fears. In fact, just two years prior, she had an opportunity to transfer to an assignment that would have allowed her to return home every day and totally eliminate all overnight travel. When faced with this opportunity, Daniel not only failed to mention his fears or concerns but he told Christina that he didn't really care one way or the other and then encouraged her to make whatever choice she wanted. He avoided possible confrontation and buried his true feelings. He thought that he could hide how he felt, and he took the easy way out by avoiding confrontation.

Had Daniel been honest with her about these feelings, she would have chosen the local assignment and they may never have gotten to the point of divorce. This bitterness and suspicion he was harboring became the springboard that launched many additional challenges in their marriage and ultimately led to their divorce.

Remember this key point: decisions and choices we make today have consequences that may not manifest themselves for months or even years to come. Sometimes, it's the things we avoid talking about or the problems we hide that are the ones that cause a small chink in our armor and weaken our relationship. What could be handled with relative ease when it is a small flame has the potential to explode into a firestorm that cannot easily be quenched.

We have a rule at work that we refer to as the "Five-Minute Rule." It simply says that if a task can be completed in five minutes or less, it should be done immediately, rather than written down and planned out in the daily or weekly work board. These small tasks can frequently grow into large assignments requiring additional man-hours to accomplish if they are put off until later. Many people like to procrastinate and put off tasks that are small or simple. If addressed or completed immediately, it results in an overall lower payroll cost. When people choose a delayed response, these small tasks multiply; and when combined with other seemingly small tasks or issues, they can become an overwhelmingly daunting task, which takes more time and effort to address.

The same is true of relationships. Things often come up that need to be addressed or discussed that would require very little time and effort if addressed immediately, but if avoided or ignored, they can grow into major problems. Don't allow yourself to ignore the seemingly small things in your relationship, hoping that they will just go away. Make a conscious effort to address these little things going forward, to avoid larger problems or confrontations down the road. This is one simple way you can choose to love your spouse each and every day.

Don't be surprised, but if you find yourself in a marriage that is unfulfilling, more than likely your spouse feels the same way. It is rare for one person to feel unfulfilled in a marriage while the other thinks that the marriage is strong and vibrant. Most likely, you have both created barriers to communication and growth, and you have both allowed your marriage to get to this point.

Just as you cannot develop an amazing marriage overnight, your marriage did not deteriorate overnight. Perhaps you just didn't see the subtle changes as they happened. It may have begun with small annoyances, or small things your spouse doesn't do that you think should be done. Perhaps you drifted apart, both becoming engrossed in work or hobbies, and you found that you were spending less and less quality time together. Perhaps it was your children, your friends, or sports activities that began taking your attention away from each other.

It is all too easy to become engrossed in a hobby or activity that seems harmless to your relationship in the beginning, but as your interest grows and the time and financial factors increase, you may discover that the very thing you enjoy doing so much is causing a strain on your relationship. If this is where you find yourself, you may be faced with another choice. Do you continue as you are with your hobby or activity, or do

No priority

you consider how to adjust your schedule to ensure your marriage has a higher priority?

We don't want to discourage you from having separate hobbies or different interests. You are who you are, and you need to have time to enjoy your hobbies. In fact, some couples tell us that their hobbies play an important role in their marriage, as it gives them some time spent either alone or with others, which makes them value the time shared with their spouse even more. We encourage you to make good choices in regard to how much time you spend pursuing your personal hobbies and interests and how much time you devote to your spouse and family. This is another choice we all need to make and one way in which our daily choices demonstrate our love and commitment to our spouse and family.

Family Choices

One choice that many couples face is whether or not both spouses should work outside of the home. This is typically not a very difficult decision, that is, until you bring children into the world. Those of you who have kids can all agree on this one thing—everything changes with kids! While it was most likely a natural thing for both of you to work before kids entered the equation, it is a very difficult decision for many couples once the kids arrive.

In our experience in talking with married couples, this is one of the hot topics that leads to emotional distress and conflict in marriage. The necessity of both spouses working can lead to a very complex decision you will need to make. Should both spouses work after the child is born? Unfortunately, this is not a decision that we can make for you, nor should it be. Every situation is different. Each circumstance will need to be discussed at length, and then an educated decision can be made after discussing both the advantages and disadvantages.

When we had our first daughter, Debby was attending a local community college and was working as a legal secretary. She thoroughly enjoyed her job and returned to work shortly after our daughter was born. Our situation was one that many young parents find themselves in—having grandparents that live close by and help out with the grandchildren.

Debby's mother volunteered to watch our baby so Debby could continue to work, and this worked out very well. For six months. After six months it wasn't that her mom couldn't or wouldn't handle our baby, but her mom decided to return to work herself.

Upon hearing that news, we began looking for childcare and we enrolled our daughter in a local daycare center. That, too, worked out well, this time for about two weeks. Debby realized the very first day we dropped our daughter off at the daycare that she couldn't leave our baby to be raised by someone else.

During those first few days of daycare, we sat down to look at our family budget and began to eliminate everything we could. We cancelled our cable TV, stopped the newspaper subscription, modified our grocery budget, and planned on eating out less often. I was working as an assistant manager in a sporting goods store, making a reasonable wage; but it was not exactly a family wage. We had some very tough choices to make in those early years, but after giving her boss a two-week notice, Debby left the working world, did not finish her degree, and became a stay-at-home mom.

Was it tough? You bet it was! We bought used furniture from my sister, scraped and saved everywhere we could, and lived in a fixer-upper house for a few years. We could fill an entire chapter on horror stories about that house, which never seemed to get fixed up like we anticipated! A few years ago it was bulldozed to the ground to make way for new office buildings—good riddance!

I can recall many times we would see other people our age without kids or with dual incomes buying expensive cars, home electronics, and other frivolous things. I think we can both honestly say, though, it didn't bother us not having the toys and gadgets that some of our friends had. Sure, it would have been nice to have some extra things, but we knew then what was important to us. And looking back now, we know that keeping Debby home was the best thing we could have done for each other and for our children.

Life together was all about the choices we made. Those choices made it clear to both of us that we valued each other and that we valued our family, regardless of our financial status. I often laugh whenever the subject of "being rich" comes up because we have frequently told our kids over the years that we are, indeed, a rich family. Rich in family love! They remind us of that often and we have a good laugh together.

Before we go any further, we want to very clearly say that keeping Debby home with our kids was a choice we made for our family at the time, and it may or may not be the choice that is right for you. When deciding whether Mom (or Dad) should go to work or stay at home with the kids, both Mom and Dad need to make the decision together. We certainly can't make that decision for you, nor can we tell you what is right for your situation. There are countless examples of couples who both have full-time jobs and maintain a healthy relationship with one another and their children.

What we will suggest, however, is that you talk about it thoroughly. Write out a budget with only one income and compare it to a budget with both parents working. The dual-income budget would need to include not only the daycare costs, but all of the costs related to having a job. This could include the cost of owning, insuring, and operating a second vehicle, the cost of clothing for the particular profession, the cost of meals while working, and any other expense that would be incurred if both parents worked outside the home.

Too often a couple will sit down and look at the amount of money an additional job will bring in, and only deduct the actual cost of daycare. Several months into the new job, they discover all these other related expenses and decide that the additional job is not providing the level of income they anticipated. They may feel that they made a poor choice but are unable to reverse course, and that's when problems begin to develop.

For some couples, you may find that having only one spouse working outside the home will provide a sufficient income for your family and any additional income the other spouse could provide is not needed. For others, you may find that you need dual incomes for the quality of life you choose to live. In addition, still others may be struggling to meet the basic financial requirements even with both parents working.

These are decisions and choices that you need to make together, as a couple. If one spouse insists on a particular choice and you are not in agreement, at some point you will ultimately pay a high price for that decision in terms of your relationship. Take the time to discuss these options in detail and come to an understanding and an agreement that you can both support. Forcing a spouse to work or to stay at home can often lead to resentment, anger, bitterness, and a host of other problems that may cause irrevocable damage to your relationship.

You may find that you both need to compromise somewhat to come to an agreement. You will find that sacrifice is always required. The sacrifice for you may be the size of your home, the neighborhood you live in, or the age and condition of your car. Or, you may need to sacrifice the amount of time you have to spend together and your free time. One thing is certain, there is always a price to pay, and sacrifice is required. Compromise is important so one spouse doesn't feel they are the one shouldering all of the sacrifice and all of the responsibility.

Remember Why You Married Him/Her in the First Place

Think back to the time you were dating or courting one another. Debby often tells people to "remember why they married their spouse in the first place." What was it about him or her that made your heart flutter and made you feel as if you couldn't live your life without that person? What caused you to spend hours with one another on the phone, sometimes without even saying anything at all? Can you remember that special song, your favorite place to eat, or something else that reminds you of the times leading up to your engagement?

What was it that made you pursue a relationship? If we asked one hundred people what they recall as the most important or dominating reason they pursued a relationship with their spouse, we'd get a variety of answers. For some, it may have started out purely as a physical attraction. For others, maybe it was an intellectual connection or a shared interest. Perhaps you met on a chance encounter, or maybe you worked together at a job. How you met isn't really what's important. What is important is what caused you to meet again. And again and again and again.

Were you the hunted or the hunter? In either case, there was an initial spark that led to a flame that grew to the fiery bonfire of passion on your wedding day. REO Speedwagon has a popular song that says "I can't fight this feeling any longer . . ." Do you remember that feeling? Do you remember what it felt like to pursue your spouse, or to be pursued by him or her?

Debby and I met under rather unusual circumstances. I was casually dating a girl, I'll call her Melinda, and there was a dance at the local roller-skating rink on a Friday night. I liked Melinda enough to want to go to the dance with her, but I was not committed enough to the relationship to pick her up or take her home afterward. In other words, as bad as it sounds, I wanted to keep my options open. I called Melinda and we arranged to meet at the dance at a specific time.

While I was sitting in my truck in the parking lot, Debby drove up in her car and pulled into the parking space facing me. We both sat there for a few minutes before she got out of her car and walked up to my truck. As I rolled down my window to see what she wanted, she asked, "Are you Jason Coleman?"

Debby had a friend who liked my best friend at the time, so she knew who I was and knew a little bit about me. Of course, I was excited and my ego spiked as this stranger knew who I was, and so we talked for a few moments until my date arrived. Melinda glared at me while Debby and I were talking, so I ended our conversation and followed Melinda into the dance. Throughout the night, Debby and I stole glances at one another, but we never talked or danced together. When I left the dance and got to my truck, I saw that Debby had left her phone number on my windshield. I called her the next day and the rest is history.

If you ever feel your relationship beginning to stale and you sense that the joy and thrill of being together is waning, it's time to remember once again those late night phone calls, the endless walks in the park, or that special treat you frequently shared together. It's important to reflect on your early moments together and remind yourself what it felt like to be in the initial stages of love. Love cannot be hidden or ignored, and the memory of young love warms the heart as you reflect on it. As you were dating, you must have made many choices to demonstrate your love and devotion to one another, and it's healthy to remember those moments.

For us, while we were dating, we spent a lot of time at the local Denny's restaurant, eating and talking. Money was very tight in those days, and most of our dates involved simply sharing a plate of fries and a shake and hanging out with each other or with her friends. Even now, as we drive past a Denny's or when our family eats there, we have fond memories about the early years in our relationship.

I can tell you that I love Debby more today than I did in those early years, and boy did I ever think that I loved her then! But the love I have for her now is a deeper love that has more meaning and a higher level of commitment. It's a stronger love, a better love, and a love that has been tested over time. It's a love that has been tested and pushed to the very brink of disaster and, yet, because of those tests, continues to grow and draw us closer together as time goes by.

Just the other night we were laughing about the hours we would spend on the phone while we were dating and the excuses we would use to spend even a few moments together. The countless hours spent at Denny's, just talking and getting to know each other, are high on our list of cherished memories. Remembering these and other times we spent together brings back good memories. Remembering what that initial spark felt like is a healthy part of our relationship.

I have a friend who was sharing with us the importance of what he calls "monumental moments." Monumental moments are those times that stand out in his life, times that are meaningful and important to him and his family and that leave a lasting impression on his life.

He told me of several monumental moments that he shared with his wife and kids. As I listened to him talk about them, I could sense a change in his voice, and I could see excitement on his face as he recalled some of these special moments. Most of them reminded him of good times they had as a couple or a family, and brought a smile to his face and an urgency to his voice as he retold the stories. It was as if he were reliving some of those experiences. They weren't all happy moments, however. Some of them reminded him of the struggles he and his wife went through, and a lesson they learned along the way. These monumental moments, both positive and negative, helped shape the relationship that he has with his wife and children today.

What are some monumental moments in your life? Take a few moments and write some down, then share them with your spouse. If you have kids, share some of your monumental moments with them, too. It is important that you model a healthy relationship in front of your kids. Your future son- or daughter-in-law will thank you!

As I was thinking back on my relationship with Debby, I can think of many monumental moments—some full of joy, some of terrific accomplishments, but also some that were tough lessons learned, including a few that were quite painful. Moments or experiences don't always have to be good ones to be memorable and they don't always have to be positive experiences to leave a positive impact on your life.

Obviously, most of us want to reflect on the moments of joy, but I think there is also value in remembering those hard lessons that we fight through. Those tough lessons may provide guidance and direction for other tough situations we will face later in life, and we can draw solutions from them. Oftentimes it is the toughest and darkest moments in our lives that prepare us for our future and give us strength and endurance.

We all have special monumental-type memories. Sometimes it's the little things in life that make us remember a conversation, a special date, or perhaps an event that impacted us in a meaningful way. How do you memorialize these moments? What are some of the things you can do to bring these back to your memory after months and even years have passed? How do you ensure that these memories will last?

Some people scrapbook for a hobby. Then again, some people like Debby take scrapbooking to a whole different level and everything they do goes into a scrapbook. Her passion for scrapbooking was so great that we bought the entire scrapbook store . . . literally! We have since closed the store, but that was a great chapter in our life which taught us many lessons. Whether you are a novice or a seasoned veteran of scrapbooking, this hobby is an excellent way to bring back special shared memories and build monuments to remind you of those moments.

Home video nights are another excellent venue for reliving some of your monumental moments. You may not have had a camera handy during the particular moment or experience, but viewing old home movies has a way of triggering our memories and we can find ourselves recalling these moments. Some of the best times we have with our kids are around the television, watching clips of their toddler years.

During the two years that we dated and throughout the early years in our marriage, late night radio played a special part in our life. The local radio station in Seattle had a show called "Lights Out" that played love songs and dedications, and we were both raving fans. As we were dating, I called the show often enough that the host of the program, Delilah Rene, knew my voice when I called and often asked how Debby and I were doing. Delilah was an integral part of our relationship, as she always knew the perfect song to play for whatever circumstance we were in. Her show is nationally syndicated now and we still listen in as often as possible.

Every day, we have many decisions to make; in fact, oftentimes our choices almost seem endless. Here's something to consider about the freedom we have to choose. You either chose to ask her to marry you, or you chose to accept the marriage proposal. You chose to walk down an aisle together in front of God, family, and friends. You also chose "till death do us part," whether or not those were the actual words used in your vows.

Now, you must choose to remain faithful to each other and to honor that marriage covenant. The quality of your marriage is based upon the choices you and your spouse make each and every day, and it begins the moment you wake up. Choose to put him or her first in everything you do, and you will further reinforce the commitment level and the prosperity of your marriage relationship.

Biblical Perspective

As you have seen in the preceding pages, we all have many decisions to make each and every day. These choices can have a dramatic impact on your relationship with your spouse. While the phrase "they fell in love" is used liberally, the truth of the matter is that people grow to love one another, and it is a process that takes time and effort. It takes a consistent effort and a daily choice to love your spouse, to put your spouse first, and to make him, or her, the most important person in your life.

Men, the Bible tells us we are to love our wives as Christ loved the church. "Husbands, love your wives, just as Christ loved the church and gave himself up for her." Eph. 5:25 (NIV) How did Christ love the Church? According to this text, He laid his life down for her. He died, that we (the Church) may live. That, my friends, is exactly what we must be willing to do on a daily basis. Not die a physical death, though that is precisely what Christ did for us, but to be willing to put our wives first and to "die" to our own selfish desires and needs. When we love and honor our wives, and put their needs before our own, we begin to experience the fullness of our relationship.

In order for our relationship to be strong and healthy, our priorities need to be in order. If we put God first, then our spouse, and then we focus on what we need, we will experience His blessing in our life and our relationship will grow and develop. However, if we put self first, and live for "me," there will be a constant conflict as we make choices that affect the time we spend with our spouse. We cannot live for self and at the same time choose every day to put our spouse first.

The Apostle Paul gave us a good example of putting others first when he instructed us to die to self daily. "I have been crucified with Christ; it is no longer I who live, but Christ lives in me; and the life which I now live in the flesh I live by faith in the Son of God, who loved me and gave Himself for me." Galatians 2:20 (NKJV). You may be asking yourself, What, exactly, does it mean to "die to self?" What Paul is saying here is that we must crucify our sinful desires of the past and live our life for Him. We must turn from those things that are purely selfish and pleasurable for us, that cause us to be so engrossed with fulfilling our own desires that we fail to meet the needs of those whom we love. Once we begin a relationship with God through Jesus Christ, we allow Christ to live in us and through us, which changes our perspective. It is a daily effort to put Christ first in our lives, and then to live to fulfill His purpose.

One of the great ways we can show our wives that we truly love them is to show them honor. In 1 Peter 3:7 it says, "In the same way, you husbands must give honor to your wives. Treat your wife with understanding as you live together. She may be weaker than you are, but she is your equal partner in God's gift of new life. Treat her as you should so your prayers will not be hindered."

Honor—this may be one of the things most cherished by women. A man who honors his wife will lighten her workload at home, be sensitive to her needs, be considerate of her, and will respect her feelings. He will consider her perspective as he makes decisions and he will show deference to her, whenever possible.

What does it mean at the end of the verse where it says that the Lord will not hear your prayers? An intimate and close relationship with the Lord generally will produce right relationships with others. If things aren't right between us and other people that we are close to, our relationship with the Lord may not be right. Conversely, if our relationship with the Lord isn't right, our other relationships may not be right either. With strained relationships, we could be out of fellowship with God and others and our prayers may go unanswered. It's all about our attitudes and the choices we make.

Ladies, there is also a command in scripture for you. Ephesians 5:22 says, "For wives, this means submit to your own husbands as unto the Lord." In Ephesians, chapter 5, Paul talks about submitting, but I think many times this passage is used to brow-beat people into submission to authority, and it is often used to say that men are dominant over women. We don't believe that to be the case at all; we believe that in marriage, both partners are called to submit equally.

This idea of biblical submission can very easily be taken out of context or misunderstood. This does not mean that wives are to be doormats for their husbands to walk all over or use them as they see fit. It doesn't mean that men can lord over women and make demands on them. And

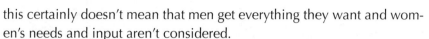
this certainly doesn't mean that men get everything they want and women's needs and input aren't considered.

As we submit to God, we willingly serve Him and allow Him to work His purpose in our lives. We submit to God's authority and we choose to serve Him. In similar fashion, wives are to follow the leading of their husband, in Christ. There is no getting around the fact that for Christians, God has placed the spiritual leadership responsibility on the husband. Quite frankly, Debby often says she is glad for that. She doesn't want to have to shoulder that responsibility. For her this is an easy concept to grasp and embrace. For others, you may see this in a different light. A factor in how women accept this fact is the manner in which her husband submits to God's authority and how he loves, honors, and respects his wife.

> Love is not a feeling or an emotion; true love is a decision.

In a Christ-centered relationship, both the husband and wife are to submit, willingly. Wives are to follow the husband's lead and he is to care for her in a selfless way. If I put Debby first, and she puts me first, we have mutual goals and we both "win." You see, part of true leadership is service. Jesus gave us the ultimate example in that because He was a servant-leader. When we submit to each other (Eph. 5:21), meaning when I serve Debby's needs and she serves my needs, there is a unique bond that we have, and more often than not, we are of one accord.

When we follow these examples Paul writes about, our relationship bears fruit that others notice and want a part of. Others will see that you two have something different in your relationship when you follow the biblical principles of mutual submission. Don't be surprised when people say that there is something different about you and your relationship, and they want to know what your secret is.

Ephesians 5:21–25 shows us a marriage that is based on the practice of love, not the feelings associated with love. Love is not a feeling or an emotion; true love is a decision. It's a choice we make, and we all have the power to choose.

We read in 1 Peter 3:4a, "You should be known for the beauty that comes from within." As the husband honors his wife and treats her in the manner that we described above, she will show him respect, submission, and the right of authority, and that will naturally reciprocate a gentle spirit. We believe these are some of the qualities referenced in this verse.

Verse 5 continues and says, "That is the way the holy women of old made themselves beautiful. They trusted God and accepted the authority of their husbands." Wives should accept the fact that God has placed the role of authority on the shoulders of her husband and she should willingly follow him. Both spouses are equal partners in God's gift of new life and are to have a spirit of unity and purpose.

Have you ever seen the bumper sticker that says "No Jesus, No Peace—Know Jesus, Know Peace"? If you want to have the peace of God, it is of utmost importance that you have a relationship with God. Notice we didn't say "religion," we said "relationship." So what does it mean to "know Jesus?" It means to have a relationship with Him, to be a child of God. The Bible tells us that God has made a choice to love us. He created us, and loves us with a unique love that we just can't duplicate. Romans 5:8 states, "But God demonstrates his own love for us in this: While we were still sinners, Christ died for us." (NIV) Have you ever given His love that much thought? The Creator of the universe died for me and for you? Wow! Go outside and gaze up at the stars, and then consider the fact that the God of the universe who knows exactly how many stars there are in the skies, created you, loves you, and has a plan for your life.

I have been a Christian for almost 75 percent of my life, yet I am still amazed that He did all that for me, because He **chose** to love me. "Greater love has no one than this, that he lay down his life for his friends." John 15:13 (NIV) I know that the love I have for Debby cannot compare with the love God has for me, but I am committed to make the daily effort to choose to love her, and to choose to make our relationship the very best it can be. If you miss everything else in this book but you understand this one concept of choice, then you understand the basic foundation from which you can build your amazing marriage.

An extremely popular verse that is read at many wedding ceremonies comes from the Old Testament, Ecclesiastes 4:12. "Though one may be overpowered, two can defend themselves. A cord of three strands is not quickly broken." The picture here is that of a man and woman, joined together in marriage, with the third strand being God.

Alone, we can easily fall into temptation and be overcome by the world. There is strength in numbers, so the two of you together will be stronger to defend against challenges and problems than if you were alone. If God is at the center of your relationship, it certainly does not guarantee you a successful and amazing marriage, but He will help you keep your priorities in order and will help you to face the daily challenges that life throws your way.

Remember your wedding day. Think through the vows you shared. Whether they were the traditional vows or unique vows you wrote yourself, ask God to give you the strength, wisdom, and perseverance to uphold those vows and to achieve the amazing marriage He intends you to have. He can help you live out the "for better or worse" portion of your vows and will help you to grow and strengthen your relationship through the "worst" parts of life. As you read this book, pray and ask God to reveal to you areas of your life that you need to surrender to Him. Ask God to fortify your marriage and to elevate your relationship with Him and with your spouse to levels you didn't even realize were possible.

Chapter 2

Communication is the Key

"The single biggest problem in communication is the illusion that it has taken place." ~ George Bernard Shaw

Communication. What is it really? Is it simply talking to another human being? Or, is it something more. At its basic core, communication is the exchange of information. We believe that communication is one of the most important aspects of an amazing marriage. Oftentimes, it is not just the daily choices we make that are important but it is the way in which we communicate those choices to our spouse that makes the difference.

Communication can be accomplished in many ways beyond simply using words. People can communicate with spoken words, body language, tone of voice, touch, eye contact, written words, sign language, and more. In most cases, we communicate using two or more methods. For example, we may use a particular tone in our voice when we say something and we may use our hands, arms, eyebrows, or other motions to convey our meaning. You probably know people who can't seem to say anything without the use of rapid hand and arm signals. You may even find that what is said is not nearly as important as what is not said or what is expressed through body language.

I have a friend who raises his eyebrows almost constantly during a conversation. Not just a little flutter once in a while, but an all-out intentional stretching of the brows! He does it when he greets me, when he shows surprise, when he emphasizes a point, or sometimes simply "just because." In the beginning I admit that I thought he was a little weird, but as I got to know him more, I realized he is genuine and he is a positive communicator.

I began responding in kind during conversations with him and have even begun to incorporate the extreme eyebrow raise in conversations with other people that need a little extra emphasis or energy. The

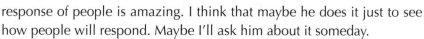

response of people is amazing. I think that maybe he does it just to see how people will respond. Maybe I'll ask him about it someday.

Another form of silent communication is the smile. A very simple gesture, a smile is universally accepted and understood. If you smile at a complete stranger, chances are very good that they will smile back. The smile transcends generational, economic, and racial barriers, and it is given freely. And when it is given, it is usually received back! Imagine if all investments paid off like the simple investment of a smile.

Our family spends a great amount of time in the car, running our four kids around town for school, sports, church, etc. Debby likes to smile at people when we stop at intersections, just to see how they respond. Most people initially look at her as if she's crazy, and then they try and figure out if they recognize her. In the end, they usually smile back. You can almost see them go through these steps in a matter of seconds. I wonder how many frustrated people are out there because the light changed to green before they figured out if they knew her or not!

A well-timed smile directed to your spouse speaks volumes. It conveys "I love you" or "I sympathize with you" or any number of encouraging messages. If you don't make it a point to smile frequently, I challenge you to try it. It changes attitudes and positively impacts those around you.

The main form of communication between couples, of course, begins with a verbal exchange. There are several outcomes of verbal communication. There are the actual words spoken, the words that are heard, the inference of the words spoken, the interpretation of the words heard, the body language expressed by the speaker, the body language as interpreted by the listener, and of course, the assumption of what was not said. The basis of it all is perspective. Zig Ziglar has spoken many times on the subject of communication, and often accentuates that what is *not* said is usually more important than what *is* said.

In chapter 1, we suggested that you and your spouse write out and discuss your goals. In this chapter, we would like to encourage you to have another discussion together. Have an open and honest discussion about where your marriage relationship is and where you'd like it to be. Are you happy with the current status of your relationship? Are you content with what could be described as the status quo? If you are not fulfilled, what are some things you would like to change or improve that would elevate your relationship to the next level? We would also like you to evaluate your intimacy. Are there some things you can do to bring more intimacy and romance into your marriage? These are topics that couples often shy away from discussing, but topics that are important to maintaining a healthy relationship.

If there are things you both would like to improve, and chances are good that there will be, make some conscious decisions to change and improve in these areas! If the problem areas are not identified, they cannot be remedied. A healthy relationship constantly undergoes evaluation and improvements to stay healthy and vibrant.

A primary rule for this discussion is that you cannot talk in an attacking manner. Respect, first and foremost, must be the priority. You cannot say "you need to change this" or "you need to do that." This is apt to cause your spouse to take a defensive position and he or she may not be open to hearing your opinion.

Keep in mind that your spouse is the person you chose to spend the rest of your life with. Tearing him or her down will not make anything better. The goal here is to identify some areas where you can take your relationship to a higher level, and you need to be careful not to destroy it in the process. It may not always be easy, but speak the truth with love and respect.

Plan a date night and select a place conducive to a good discussion. If you have a history of not being able to discuss tough subjects without getting angry at one another and fighting, choose a public location. Choose somewhere private enough to be able to talk without interruption or embarrassment of being overheard, but public enough to hold yourself in check so you don't get angry and say things you may regret.

For this process, each spouse writes a list of things that are important in the marriage. The husband creates his list of what is important and the wife does the same. When the lists are finished, compare the lists and ask each other, "If I do these things for you, will this add value to you and demonstrate love? Will it show you that I am committed to making our marriage amazing and that I am committed to meeting your needs in this process?" Remember that consciously deciding each and every day that your marriage will be amazing is the most important step in reaching the goal.

As you share what is important to you and then begin to discuss the things you want to see changed, begin with statements such as, "I'd like to go out on a date once a month" or "I would like to see intimacy and romance become a higher priority in our marriage" or "I'd like to be able to carve out some time each week, just for the two of us."

Statements such as these aren't accusatory or demeaning. Notice you didn't say, "We never go out anymore" or "You never want to have sex as often as you used to" or "You're never home, and when you are you're always doing your own thing—it's like when you are here physically you are absent emotionally." These types of statements are sure to generate a defensive response and could lead to your spouse shutting down before the discussion even begins in earnest.

It may be true that the two of you never go out on dates anymore, and perhaps the sex isn't as frequent as it once was, and maybe he or she is preoccupied when they are home and there is no quality time spent together anymore. These are definitely things that you want to see changed, but it would be much more productive to phrase your concerns in a positive and nonthreatening manner. Rather than point out the problem, try to provide solutions without your spouse having to feel bad for not meeting your needs.

As you discuss your list, be sure to speak for yourself and allow your spouse to speak for him- or herself. What we mean by that is say what you truly mean and explain how you feel. You need to have the freedom to talk openly and honestly with each other, regardless of what you think your spouse may want to hear. If you say what you think they would expect you to say and you aren't true to your feelings, how could you expect to make changes in your marriage? Honesty is of utmost importance during this discussion.

Before you open this dialogue, we recommend you set the ground rules for discussion. We have found this to be a very important aspect of sharing together, particularly when you are discussing potential challenges in your relationship. One ground rule that should be set and respected by both of you is that only one of you speaks at a time. When you or your spouse is talking, the other cannot interrupt. It is important to allow your spouse to finish their train of thought before you jump in with your rebuttal or opinion.

You may each want to have a pad of paper with you during this time so you can take notes, but you cannot interrupt, no matter how tempting it is to do so. Also, your notes are not for the sake of arguing every point that was made, but so you can refer back to something your spouse has said if it requires additional dialogue or clarification. Keep in mind, this isn't a boxing ring so you don't need to land a punch for every point you don't agree with.

Of all the different aspects of communication, one that is often overlooked is the ability to listen. When your spouse is talking, be sure to be attentive. Be a good listener, and most importantly, do not interrupt. Truly listening and hearing what is being communicated is a skill that is not easily mastered. One of my favorite quotes on communication is, "The one who listens controls the outcome of the conversation."

> Merely knowing that the need exists doesn't meet the need; you must take action.

This is important, because if you truly desire to make changes in your marriage, you need to take the responsibility to initiate change yourself. If you don't listen to what your spouse says or needs, you will not know where to begin to initiate the necessary changes.

If you develop good listening habits, you will be demonstrating to your spouse your commitment to the marriage and your desire to make the necessary changes and improvements. If your relationship is on rocky ground and your spouse doesn't believe you are sincere about making improvements, this is a good way to start. When we choose to listen, we choose to add value to our spouse and give them the respect their opinion deserves.

As you both discuss your lists, you will most likely hear, or use the phrase "I feel . . ." It is important that you respect each other's feelings and validate those feelings. You may have a different opinion and you may not agree on how he or she feels, but realize that they feel that way for a reason, and you need to validate and acknowledge their feelings.

Once each of you has shared your list and you know what it is that you and your spouse need and want, slowly begin to incorporate those needs and desires into your daily life. Whether it's a quiet dinner out more often, more frequent or fulfilling sex, a love note, a gift, a helping hand around the house, a quiet walk . . . whatever it is, make a conscious decision every day to do a little bit to show your spouse your love and commitment.

Another important aspect to remember is that words are hollow if not acted upon. As you develop an understanding of what your spouse feels is missing from your marriage, follow through on what your spouse wants, and start the process of meeting those needs. Merely knowing that the need exists doesn't meet the need; you must take action.

Look for opportunities to surprise your spouse. If it's a note of appreciation she needs, and you're not sure what to write, start small. Perhaps you leave a sticky-note posted on the refrigerator or the computer monitor. A simple "Thanks for all you do. I Love You," is a great place to start. A gift card for a favorite store is always appreciated and could be a great way to show appreciation. A card with a heartfelt expression of your love and scented with a favorite cologne will mean more than you can imagine.

Words of affirmation are important to Debby. If there is one thing I wish I would have done more often in our early years, it is sending her a love letter on a frequent basis. Not regular, so she comes to expect them, but randomly frequent. She has a box hidden away of all the cards and letters I wrote when we were dating and engaged (and yes, there were some after we married, too; just not as many). As I read them on occasion, I have a hard time figuring out how I was able to pen such poetic beauty. It must be the magic of new love.

Fast-forward to present day life. If there's something I want Debby to see or if I need to leave her a message, it always goes in front of the coffee pot. This way I know, beyond a shadow of doubt, that she will get it. It's the first thing she goes to in the morning, and she visits the coffee pot often throughout the day. Regardless of the time of day or night, it's a safe bet that she will get a message left there.

One day as we began writing the outline for this portion of the book, I wrote a small "I Love You" note for Debby. I folded it up small and hid it in the can of coffee grounds. I had no idea when she would discover it, but when she found it, one of our teenage daughters was in the kitchen. She read it after Debby said something to the effect of, "Oh, that's so sweet!" And our daughter said, "Oh my gosh, he put that in the coffee? Dad needs to give lessons on how to be a boyfriend. He sets the standard way too high! How am I going to find a guy like him?"

You see, it's often the little things we do for each other that make a big difference and leave a lasting impression. In this case, I was able to leave an impression on both my wife and my daughter! Our daughter needs to know what to expect from a husband and she deserves to have the bar of excellence set high.

I remember very clearly in the early years of our marriage how we struggled to communicate with one another. We would both allow feelings to build up inside until they boiled over. We didn't talk about things that bothered us and tried to avoid difficult topics. Almost without fail, we would have a drag-down, no-holds-barred fight about every three months.

Like clockwork, we would get to a point where we couldn't hold everything in anymore and we would unleash a barrage after barrage of anger at each other, like an artillery bombardment preceding an invasion. Usually it would be a very small offense or disagreement that started the argument, but the pent-up anger would spill over and we would move on to other topics, almost never resolving or even remembering the initial disagreement.

One thing Debby would typically say at some point in our fight was, "I can't do it all." That would undoubtedly be followed with "You're always gone at work and you're never here. You don't help with the girls. You don't cook or clean. You don't help with the laundry. You don't . . . you don't . . . and you don't. . . ." Of course, this is when I would get exceedingly defensive and I would dig in and prepare myself for battle.

It is important to avoid using words such as "never" or "always" when having discussions. These blanket statements imply a much broader meaning than you probably intend and they are rarely truthful statements. It would be highly unlikely that your spouse "never" or "always" does or says something and their response to hearing these words is like throwing gasoline on a fire. Nothing good comes from stoking the fiery emotions of your spouse during an argument.

After accusing me of being selfish and not fulfilling my household duties, she would cry and then start in with the "You never buy me things anymore" and "You don't send me flowers or love letters anymore." It would go on like this for several minutes as she would remind me of all the things I "used to do" and all the things I should be doing. Of course, she would remind me of these things in a very threatening and accusatory manner.

After my anger subsided and my defenses were spent, I would immediately think to myself that I would need to write a note or send flowers, but that I'd have to wait a few days. I mean, if I sent flowers the very next day she'd think I was only sending them because we fought. I thought it wouldn't mean anything to her. It would be almost like she expected it. So, as it usually turned out, I would wait a few days, but then I would forget and I'd never send the flowers or write the note.

Then, because we didn't know how to communicate and get ourselves out of the rut we were in, she would throw that out at me in our next fight three months later! I still didn't buy her anything special or send love notes! It was a never ending cycle that was spiraling out of control. We needed help, but we didn't know what to do or where to turn.

What I should have done was to buy those flowers for her the very next day. I should have taken immediate action, as a validation of her feelings, and then made a reminder of some sort to myself to write a note and leave it for her a few days after that. But because I didn't realize that I had to make a conscious choice every day to love her in a demonstrative way, we remained in that rut for nearly two years. A mentor of mine used to say that a rut is simply a grave with the ends kicked out. If we were going to break the cycle of fighting and save our marriage, we needed to take some drastic measures before the grave was filled in and we were buried, with no options left other than to fight it out in divorce court.

For us, help came through some friendships. I asked for a job transfer within my company and we left Washington State in 1993 and moved to Phoenix, Arizona. At that point in time we had weathered some pretty serious storms in our relationship, including a near-disastrous affair. We both thought that if we got away from the influence of our parents and others, we would be forced to rely on each other and make it on our own. Looking back, we don't necessarily disagree with that concept, but we know that it takes much more than simply moving away and being forced to rely on one another to succeed and build your marriage relationship.

We moved to Phoenix with our two daughters and we had a pretty good first year. Our relationship had the normal amount of ups and downs, perhaps maybe more downs than ups due to the fact that we were in a new environment. We had some family support in Phoenix, as my father and his second wife lived there as well as my grandparents and an aunt and uncles, but we didn't seek out much in the way of emotional or relationship support from any of the family there. My father's marriage was crumbling, which was of no help or encouragement for us.

I clearly recall one Sunday morning in Phoenix, after we had endured a couple of very difficult cycles of these three-month fights, we were standing in a church service and while the congregation was singing I suddenly began to cry uncontrollably. I do not recall what the song was, but there I stood completely sobbing like a baby. Not being able to hide it, and yet not wanting to draw any additional attention to myself, I quickly left and went back to the men's bathroom where I remember just crying for what seemed to be a very long time.

Several men in the congregation had seen me leave and came into the bathroom to see what was wrong. I couldn't stop crying and couldn't speak for quite some time. When the sobbing slowed down enough for me to breathe controllably and talk, I clearly remember telling one of the men, Harold, that my marriage was going to end if I didn't do something drastic.

I don't recall knowing this at the time, but Harold was a licensed counselor who was in seminary to be a pastor. He was exactly the guy I needed to talk to that day. We set up a schedule of counseling sessions, both one-on-one with him and me and then also together with Debby. Harold may not realize it, but he was an important influence on us, and our marriage may not have survived without his intervention.

Harold taught me how to listen, how to truly listen to Debby, and we both learned how to communicate our feelings to each other. I also learned how to validate her feelings. These are basic fundamental aspects of communication in our marriage that we can point to as keys in our relationship that we utilize time and time again.

Just like sending that note or buying flowers should have been my immediate response, immediate action goes both ways. Unless the husband and wife both commit to making changes and improvements, it just won't work. One spouse making the changes and putting forth all the effort and the other spouse reaping the benefit will eventually cause bitterness, anger, and resentment in the spouse that is investing in the marriage. In addition, the spouse doing all the work may just give up and "settle" once again for mediocrity in the marriage. However, if you want to make changes but your spouse is indifferent or doesn't realize changes need to be made, don't let this hold you back. Initiate the changes you can, and over time your spouse will begin to take notice and should begin to respond.

We want to stress that it takes hard work on the part of both of you to create an amazing marriage. It won't happen overnight, in a month, or even in a year. It takes time; a tremendous amount of time. For us, it took many years. Over time, trust will build and develop, your communication will improve, and before you know it people will begin asking you what it is that you have that is so special.

People close to you will notice the difference and ask what you have done. They will see that the two of you are different than most couples and that you have a unique relationship, and they will want to experience for themselves what you have. When that happens, you may be able to become a Harold for someone who needs encouragement in their relationship.

All of the changes that need to be made in your relationship won't necessarily need to be drastic, but they do need to be consistent. These changes will be different for each couple, so we can't give you a one-size-fits-all solution, but you can find one thing to start with—that you could do immediately and at no cost—that will have a direct impact on your relationship. Start small, but start today. John C. Maxwell says that you will never change your life until you change something you do on a daily basis. Identify a place to start, and initiate that change. Change is an ongoing process and will evolve over time.

As you begin to implement changes, sometimes the results will be immediate and other times you may wonder if your spouse is even noticing your effort. Oftentimes you may not see any improvements for an extended period of time. Don't let that discourage you. If things have been difficult for years, your spouse may not trust the changes you are making and may not respond. He or she may be filled with so much anger and doubt that it takes time for you to prove your intentions are worthy. Persevere and be consistent. Stay the course. Pause for a moment and think of some things you can do today that will make your spouse feel more loved, more appreciated, or perhaps more respected. Write a few ideas down and begin to implement them today.

If you have not yet begun this process with your spouse and have not had the dialogue we are suggesting, you can still put this idea into action immediately. He or she may not even be aware of your concerns with your marriage, or may even be convinced that you don't really care about where your relationship is headed. This effort on your part may be the catalyst that will demonstrate to your spouse your desire to make changes and improvements in your marriage. This may be the launching point for real and lasting change.

On the other hand, perhaps your relationship is strong and thriving. You can still evaluate your relationship and identify areas where you can make changes. Even the best of relationships can be improved and elevated to a higher level of commitment and love.

~

Remember Amy, from the Foreword of this book? Amy is concerned that her marriage is failing, but Thomas doesn't seem to think they have a problem. In fact, he tries to put on a façade that everything is fine and they are doing well. He fails to admit or recognize the fact that their relationship is lacking the intimacy and closeness they once shared. Until he acknowledges her feelings and they have a discussion to identify her concerns, Amy and Thomas will either be on a collision course toward a failed marriage or, at best, they will endure an unfulfilled relationship.

For me, identifying something that I could do to make Debby feel more loved and appreciated is pretty simple. For example, one thing she would always say at some point during our quarterly fights was "I can't do it all." By making time to help out around the house, I was able to show her in a tangible way that I desired to make improvements in our relationship. It may sound too simplistic to some of you, but the simple task of doing dishes or folding laundry was a way of adding value to my wife. My only regret is that I didn't recognize this earlier in our marriage.

Now, if I take it to the next level and actually *put away* the folded laundry, it means that much more. For a family of six, we seem to generate an inordinate amount of laundry each week. Of course, seeing shirts perfectly folded lying in the dirty laundry basket among wadded up clothing doesn't help the situation much. Debby's frustration level understandably goes up when our children don't take the time to put their folded laundry away and it winds up in the laundry basket again!

I discovered over time that if I would set aside time to help with the daily routines of managing the household, separating laundry, washing dishes, running car-pool, etc., I was adding value to Debby and showing her love and appreciation. This was a way I could choose to show her love on a daily basis. Gary Smalley has a wonderful book entitled *The Five Love Languages*. If you can discover what your spouse's love language is and learn to speak that language, you will be well on your way to adding value to your spouse and will be on the path toward having an amazing marriage.

Kenny Rogers released a song in late 1999 titled "Buy Me a Rose" on his *She Rides With Wild Horses* album. In the song he talks about a husband who attempts to please his wife by buying her material things, such as a three-car garage and a credit card of her own. The song describes how she feels all alone and really just wants him to show her his love, but through his attention and actions, not through materialistic gifts. At the end of the song he reveals that the woman is his own wife and he finally learns what she really wants. He pledges to do all of these things for the rest of their lives.

This song could have been written about me. In fact, the way the husband was described in the beginning of the song still is me sometimes. I know I need to make a continuous effort to remember to do the little things for Debby. Every day I make an effort to do these little things, because I know that it is something she responds to. A rose, a card, or some sort of appreciation goes a long way with her. I still don't get it right all the time, but relationships are always in motion and require a consistent and daily effort.

Decision Making

With regard to financial decisions, we suggest that you set a monetary limit on your spending. Now this isn't a ground-shattering new idea of ours, but it is a very important part of the relationship that we feel we must address. For us, a good spending limit is twenty-five dollars.

Prior to making any personal (or even family) purchase over twenty-five dollars, we call each other and talk about it. It's not a matter of getting permission; rather, it's a matter of respecting each other and respecting the family budget enough to be sure that the purchase can be afforded without using credit, and that it's an expense the family budget can tolerate. If those two things are okay, then it's a reasonable purchase. If the purchase must be done on credit, it is something we always discuss beforehand.

This spending limit has kept us from making impulsive purchases that we wanted at the time, but knew we couldn't afford. Having this agreement in place has meant that we have been able to stay out of some of the serious problems that impulsive spending can create. Unfortunately, money, or more correctly, the perceived lack of money, is a major contributing factor to marital problems.

Notice that we phrased it as the "perceived" lack of money. We have known many couples who struggle with their finances and continually sink deeper and deeper into debt while continuing to live beyond their means. We have friends who live in apartments or homes they can't afford, drive cars with monthly payments beyond their means, have cable or satellite television and multiple cell phones, all while struggling to make the minimum payments on their credit cards. You undoubtedly know people that fit this description as well.

Rather than cancel the cable and reduce the monthly cell phone use, or even eliminate the cell phone altogether, they make these payments with a credit card and wonder why they just can't seem to get ahead. There are usually a number of frivolous expenses that can be cut out of most budgets, but many couples lack the discipline to make the cuts.

I have been in the retail sporting goods industry for over twenty years, and I often tell the young up-and-coming management prospects that the sporting goods industry can be summed up in a simple phrase: People buy things they can't afford, with money they don't have, to impress people that just don't care. Unfortunately, that isn't just true of the sporting goods industry!

Here's an example of the dangers of credit. According to Bankrate. com, if you have a balance on a credit card of $5,000, with a modest 12% APR, it will take over twenty-three years to pay it off if you only make the minimum payment! In addition, you will end up paying $4,545 in interest, resulting in a total payoff of $9,545 for that $5,000 balance! Even if you manage to obtain a 6% APR, it will still take you over fifteen years to pay off the balance at a total cost of $1,531 in interest.[1] Credit card companies set the minimum payment low in an effort to keep you in debt as long as possible if you only pay the minimum amount due.

Several times over the years circumstances have required us to use credit more than we wanted to because we didn't have the habit of saving money for emergencies. As we dig ourselves out of debt, rather than simply paying the minimum amount due on our credit cards, we focus on paying off the account with the lowest balance first. We apply as much additional money as we can onto the minimum payment for that account. When that balance is retired, we add the amount of money we

---

1 http://www.bankrate.com/calculators/managing-debt/minimum-payment-calculator.aspx

had been paying on that account to the next lowest balance. By doing this, we accelerate the process and minimize the time it takes to get out of debt. We also save money on interest payments by reducing the balance owed at a faster rate.

As you establish a spending limit, each couple will have a different dollar amount based on their own unique budget and circumstances. We set the twenty-five-dollar limit in our first year of marriage when a large purchase would drastically impact our monthly budget, and we have stayed with it for many years. Several years ago we increased that amount based on the fact that we are in a better financial position than we were when we first were married, but the important issue is that we communicate with each other and we made this decision together.

If this is the approach you choose to take, you should also communicate purchases for the special occasions in your life. Whether your budget is tight or not, if you deviate from this agreement for birthdays or holidays, you will find yourself in deeper financial problems, which may be a root cause for problems in many marriages today.

We have a great example of the importance of watching finances for special occasions. When we were married, I was twenty-two and Debby was eighteen. When we were deciding when to set the date for our wedding, we decided on the Saturday that fell between our birthdays. We didn't realize it at the time, but this decision wreaked financial havoc in the early years of our marriage. You see, our birthdays are only one week apart. Our anniversary is right in between the two birthdays so that means we have three very special occasions within one week of each other. Early in our marriage we did everything we could to celebrate all three occasions, which meant taking on debt. As you can probably imagine, this tore into our family budget! We tried this unsuccessfully for a few years.

When we made the commitment to be more fiscally responsible and accountable to each other, we made the decision to celebrate our birthdays and anniversary on alternating years. Once this decision was made it was such a relief. The pressure was off as far as buying something "big" for all occasions. This was a huge step for both of us and a huge leap forward with our home budget. We determined that compromise for the sake of the family budget worked perfectly in this instance. It is easy to justify a purchase for a special occasion, but when the electric bill is due and you don't have the money in the checking account, that special purchase may not seem as important as it did at the time.

~

Jason has been writing up to this point, but I (Debby) want to write this specifically from my perspective. In our marriage, I don't want the authority of the final decisions. Whether it's financial, something with the kids, a new pet, or virtually anything to do with our lives or marriage, Jason has the final word. That's not to say that I don't voice my opinion or that I just concede to every wish and desire of his, but that the ultimate decision is his.

We always set aside a time to discuss an issue or any major purchase. I state my opinion, and if it involves the entire family, we include the kids in the discussion. We want them to know that we value their opinion. Anyone in our family has the right to call a family meeting at any time and for any reason. I state my opinion and Jason disseminates my thoughts, desires, and needs before making the final decision. When the decision is made, it is final. If I neglect to put my opinion or thoughts out there, I don't feel that I can question or argue the decision after it's been made.

There was a time, early in our marriage, that Jason made a final decision with regards to a family move. He ultimately made a decision that was against what I suggested and wanted and we sold our house in Phoenix, Arizona and moved to Albuquerque, New Mexico. I am embarrassed to share that for years after he made that decision I was relentless to remind him how unhappy I was and what a poor decision I thought he made. I truly have no idea how he put up with me as kindly as he did. Many years later, I was able to look back and realize that he did make the right decision, and I was just too selfish and narrow-minded to see it.

I was finally able to think beyond myself and look at the big picture. I appreciate that Jason is willing to make these final decisions. He understands his role as my husband and the leader in my life, and he takes it very seriously. He respects me and I know, beyond a shadow of a doubt, that he has my best interest and the interest of our family at heart when making decisions. Because of our mutual trust and respect, I know he will make decisions that are best for our family. With that said, I'll hand the pen back to Jason now.

~

On those occasions where a bad decision was made, and some bad ones have been made, we all support it and live with the consequences, but we do so without assigning blame. As we have already said, an amazing marriage is not a perfect marriage, and when decisions turn out poorly and the end results are contrary to expectations, we make the best of the situation. We work through disappointments and setbacks together.

We have had more than our fair share of financial problems over the years and have made numerous mistakes, learning in the process almost enough to include an entire chapter on finances. The key to financial security is not dependent on how much money you make, but how you manage it.

The secret to financial security is spending within your means. In other words, creating a budget for your income level and sticking to it, or spend less than you make. It's a pretty simple concept, really. In this day and age that we live in, though, too many of us are concerned with what other people have compared to what we have, and as we try to "keep up with the Joneses" we mortgage our future. My mentor loved this quote, "Pay now or pay later, but remember that if you pay later, you always pay more." How true this is in many different aspects of our lives.

If you are not currently living on a budget, let us encourage you to develop one as soon as possible. There are many excellent resources to help you write a financially responsible budget, you just need to make the decision and have the commitment to stick with it. The fear of starting a budget that you may not be able to live on may be the biggest stumbling block there is for living within your means. Many people are afraid that they can't live on a budget, so they never formulate a budget, and then they have no idea where all of their money goes each month.

Having a responsible budget that you follow may help eliminate many fights about money, as you will both know where the money is being spent. It is important that you communicate about money and that you both agree on your budget. You need to know how much income you have, what your fiscal responsibilities are, and how you are allocating your money. You will both need to be in agreement in regards to spending and saving money, as well as your financial goals.

Selfless vs. Selfish

I have to take the pen back from Jason for this topic. If I get to a point when I think I may be unhappy in my marriage, the first thing I do is evaluate my attitude. Usually it is evident that I am critical of Jason. Thoughts about the things he isn't doing for me—or what I think he should be doing for me—flood my mind. I tend to dwell on thoughts of why I'm unhappy and unfulfilled and how Jason is falling short of my expectations (we discuss unmet expectations in chapter 6). When I realize how unhappy I am, I begin to reevaluate my attitude and ask myself why I feel this way.

When I do that, I always come back to the same thought: I am too focused on self and am thinking too much about me. The more I focus on me, the more frustrated I become. It's so easy to fall into this trap. Our society seems to be focused on self. We focus on self-improvement, self-esteem, self worth, self-fulfillment, and there is even an entire magazine dedicated to *Self*. The idea of "self" permeates our lives through the various forms of media and bombards our society with the goal of taking care of Numero Uno.

I have realized through the years that when I put Jason's needs before mine I am much happier. When I can see his needs being met and he is content in our marriage, the happier I am. It's a strange phenomenon, indeed, but it rings true year after year. When I concentrate on Jason and put him before myself, it brings me joy. I'm not unhappy for myself when I fulfill his needs. I find that I am too busy meeting his needs to be dwelling on myself; therefore, I am content and fulfilled.

The more I focus on Jason and make sure his needs are met, the more he focuses on me and meets my needs. The world tells us to take care of self first, but I find that I am actually happier taking care of his needs, because I know my needs will be met as well.

This is called reciprocation, or the law of reciprocity. The basic premise is that the good that I do for my husband comes back to me, and usually the return is greater. However, the opposite is also true. When I fail to meet his needs or he fails to meet mine, over time this is also reciprocal and we find ourselves needing to reassess our priorities. It is important that you meet the needs of your spouse the way he or she needs them to be met; not the way you think they should be met.

Affirming vs. Assaulting

One thing that really breaks our hearts is to hear a husband or wife verbally tear down their spouse, and it is especially disturbing to us when we witness this in a public setting. I have a friend who has so much

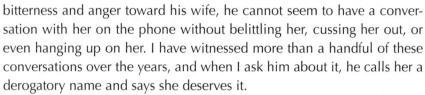
bitterness and anger toward his wife, he cannot seem to have a conversation with her on the phone without belittling her, cussing her out, or even hanging up on her. I have witnessed more than a handful of these conversations over the years, and when I ask him about it, he calls her a derogatory name and says she deserves it.

This same friend, I'll call him Richard, has virtually no romance in his marriage. He continually complains that his wife doesn't engage in any intimacy and fails to meet his needs, yet he fails to see that she is only responding in kind. Rather than affirm his wife, he is continually assaulting her verbally and emotionally. This has caused her to completely shut down and has driven a wedge between them that will not be easily overcome.

I have known Richard for many years and I can't remember him ever saying anything positive and encouraging to her or about her. She doesn't do this or doesn't do that, is always spending too much money, doesn't keep up the house, needs to lose weight, etc. The worst part is, he not only tells *me* these things, but I have heard him tell her specific things I would never ever say to my worst enemy. The verbal assaults continue day after day and year after year, and yet he wonders why there is no passion and romance in his marriage.

I remember one specific year when they reached their twenty-fifth wedding anniversary. This is a major milestone in any relationship and should be celebrated in a special way. He called and asked me what he should do for her, but then said in the same breath that it didn't really matter because whatever he did wouldn't mean anything to her anyway. We talked about a few ideas and I encouraged him to make it special.

I was actually quite proud of him, at first. He sent a large balloon bouquet with a teddy bear to her at work. After work he took her out for a nice dinner and had bought her a diamond necklace, which cost around eight hundred dollars. He made a good effort to plan out a nice evening for just the two of them.

You can imagine his disappointment when she didn't reciprocate with a gift of any kind. Nothing! Nada! Zip! No gift or even a card to commemorate their twenty-five years together. In addition to that, she wanted their two daughters to go to dinner with them and "had a headache" that night. He was completely shut out in the romance department. The following day I heard all about it, and, of course, according to him, it was all her fault. I'm quite certain I didn't get the entire story.

To this very day, he holds a grudge that is beyond belief and anytime this comes up in discussion, I hear the frustration and disappointment in his voice. I fear it will be a very long time before he gets beyond the hurt and rejection. The following Valentine's Day, he refused to acknowledge the day and did not give her a card or any gift.

When he got home on that Valentine's Day, she casually said, "Oh, yeah, I got something for you, it's out in my car." He was both surprised and curious, so he went out to the car to see what was there. What he found was a nineteen-inch flat screen TV. When he brought it inside the house, she said, "I won it at work yesterday, hope you like it."

Right or wrong, he took offense to that and believed that had she not won the TV, he again would have received nothing for a major holiday. The fact that she was giving him a gift that she won rather than one she picked out and purchased really upset him. It demonstrated to him that she didn't really care and didn't appreciate him.

Now, before you go thinking he is the sole responsible party for their problems, we have only heard his part of the story. I have known them both for many years, but have never had an opportunity to talk to her about their relationship. I have tried many times to explain to Richard that as long as he continues to talk to her the way he does, she will continue to respond to him the way she does. Until one of them makes a conscious decision to break the cycle, they will continue to build resentment for one another and will continue to destroy each other and their marriage.

When we choose to assault rather than affirm our spouses, our kids, our bosses, our employees, or whomever we come into contact with, we cannot expect good things to result. When we assault our spouses, whether verbally or physically, we damage the relationship and grow further and further apart.

~

Positive communication is vital to the health of your marriage. Choosing your words carefully, particularly during an argument or disagreement, is a major key to resolving your differences. Choose to speak to your spouse with respect and with words of affirmation. It is so sad to see many people treat others, even complete strangers, with more respect and courtesy than they show their own life-long mate. If you have a habit of responding with anger or negativity, make a conscious decision to

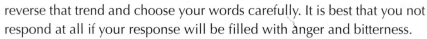

reverse that trend and choose your words carefully. It is best that you not respond at all if your response will be filled with anger and bitterness.

We see this response in our teenage daughters at times. It doesn't take much for one of them to push the other into an argument and then they both lash out with fury. They turn on each other with biting and hateful words, and an instant later be as sweet as honey to their friends.

To cultivate a relationship, we need to be genuine, loving, and respectful, and we need to treat those whom we love better than those to whom we befriend. It is very sad, indeed, when people treat complete strangers better than they treat their spouses.

~

Communication between a husband and wife must always be truthful and honest. Once trust is broken, it is extremely difficult to rebuild. So many aspects of a marriage rely on trust and honesty. We have made a commitment to love and cherish one another "till death do us part." In order to fulfill that commitment to each other, we need to rely entirely on one another. We need to be able to fully and completely trust everything our spouse says and does. If there's dishonesty and distrust, it is impossible to rely on one another during the tough times and this will cause the foundation of a relationship to erode and crumble.

Biblical Perspective

How many times do we really communicate to our wives that we truly love them? Or appreciate them? As men, we need to be aware of what our wives need. We need to be tuned into their emotions and learn to read not only what they are saying, but oftentimes what they are not saying. When we learn to effectively communicate with our wives, we add value to them and treasure them. Proverbs 18:22 says, "He who finds a wife, finds a good thing (treasure) and obtains favor with the Lord" (NKJV). Men, if you are reading this and you are married, you have found a "good thing"...now cherish her like an expensive treasure and savor the favor of the Lord!

As we indicated earlier in this chapter, find some time to discuss your goals with one another and the things you would like to see changed in your relationship. As you do this, be vulnerable enough to honestly discuss frustrations or issues that bother you. Proverbs 27: 6 says, "Wounds from a friend can be trusted, but an enemy multiplies kisses." (NIV) (Even though you are telling your spouse things he or she may not want to hear, if you do so with a gentle spirit and with the intention of bringing resolution, you should be able to discuss topics that are important to you. Ephesians 4:29 says, "Do not let any unwholesome talk come out of your mouths, but

> As a Christian, the way you handle your money says a lot about the amount of faith you have in God's provision.

only what is helpful for building others up according to their needs, that it may benefit those who listen." (NIV)

James 1:19 says, "My dear brothers and sisters, be quick to listen, slow to speak, and slow to get angry." With each conversation you have, be sure to listen intently to what is being said. One way I can honor Debby and value her is to listen to her and validate her feelings. Even if I disagree with her, if I follow the words of James and I listen before I speak, there is more harmony in our lives. This doesn't mean that I don't have my own opinions that may differ from hers; what this means is that we honor one another's opinion and respect each other.

In all that you do, encourage one another. Let your husband or wife know how much they mean to you, and encourage their individualism while promoting unity. Paul wrote, "Let us therefore make every effort to do what leads to peace and to mutual edification." (Romans 14:19) (NIV) "May the God who gives endurance and encouragement give you a spirit of unity among yourselves as you follow Christ Jesus" (Romans 15:5 NIV). Speak lovingly and with respect whenever you are with your spouse. "A word aptly spoken is like apples of gold in settings of silver." (Proverbs 25:11) (NIV)

As a Christian, the way you handle your money says a lot about the amount of faith you have in God's provision. There are numerous biblical passages concerning money and we are commanded to be good stewards of the resources God blesses us with. It is certainly not sinful or wrong to be wealthy, but God doesn't want us to be poor either. I think there are people who believe that if we don't give away everything we have and live a life of barely scraping by, that we're somehow not meeting God's expectations.

Throughout our marriage, Debby has struggled with giving consistently to the church and we haven't always agreed on how much we should give. We have seen the Lord provide for us over and over again, and I believe that He is faithful and will bless obedience. Recently Debby had a situation where she saw first hand the provision of God in a little matter which impacted her in a big way.

We currently have a balance on several credit cards and we are committed to eliminating the debt and living debt-free. One thing we are doing is using cash as much as possible for our daily living expenses, and spending only the cash we have set aside in a particular category. For example, our two-week grocery budget is two hundred and fifty dollars, and when it is spent, it is spent. Each category has a spending limit that we have designated. We have agreed not to use credit to augment our daily living expenses.

She went to the grocery store to purchase a few items for a special dinner we were having for some friends and we needed ingredients for a salad and dessert as well as a few other items. She took the last forty dollars in our grocery envelope, and had a list of what we needed. When she was at the cash register to check out, the total came to $41.74, which exceeded her cash. Previously, she would have thought nothing of pulling out her debit or credit card to make the purchase and would have put the forty dollars in her pocket for spending money.

Determined not to use the cards, she began digging in her purse to see if she could find change. She doesn't carry loose change too often and completely expected to find nothing but a few loose pennies. To her amazement, she pulled out a handful of loose change from the bottom of her purse and was excited to see that the majority of the coins were quarters, not pennies. She promptly counted out the one dollar and seventy four cents, and gleefully exclaimed, "I got it!" to the cashier and our daughter.

Because of her commitment to stay the course, honor our budget, and not use the cards, God provided for her in a way she didn't expect. For a lady who despises carrying loose change in her purse, this impacted her in a very dramatic way. God often uses little examples such as this to demonstrate His provision for us.

Chapter 3

Intimacy in Your Amazing Marriage

"Once in a while, right in the middle of an ordinary life, love gives you a fairy tale." ~ Author Unknown

Intimacy in your amazing marriage—"it" begins in the kitchen! "It" begins in the kitchen? Now you're probably thinking, does that mean what I think it means? Yes it does! Debby often says that sex begins in the kitchen. Now, we don't mean this in a literal sense, but the idea here is that in order for her to "warm up" for intimacy, she likes to think about it all day, and she needs me to value her throughout the day. She needs to see and hear certain things from me that demonstrate to her my love, and it begins in the morning. In other words, it's a day-long process.

It has often been said that a man is a microwave and a woman is an oven. Guys, think about it like this. If you come home from work, the kids are all out of the house at a sporting event or a friend's house, and your wife meets you at the door wearing a sexy lace and fur-lined outfit, you'd be ready to go immediately. Dinner would wait. The newspaper would be forgotten. The television would be ignored. You wouldn't need any urging or convincing. Lovemaking is in the air tonight!

If, however, those roles were reversed and you met your wife at the door as she returned home in a similar situation, most likely she would be more concerned with where the kids are, what's planned for dinner, who is picking up Johnny from soccer practice, did you pick up the dry cleaning, etc.? In fact, she may even think it's pretty presumptuous of you to think she would be even remotely interested in sex the moment she walks through the door.

Those of us who have been married for longer than, say, thirty seconds, realize that when it comes to sex and romance, our wives are wired differently than we are. I realize this is stereotypical, and that there are exceptions to this, but in general men are ready to engage in sexual activity with little or no advance planning while women typically need time to prepare emotionally. If not discussed and understood, this difference can cause significant problems in a relationship. I remember in our early years I would misinterpret this to think she didn't want me any more, and I would only grow angry and bitter.

• I hate to even admit this, but there were times when I felt so rejected and our relationship was pretty shaky, that I would tell myself that I could hold out longer than she could, and when the time came that she would want to have sex, I would be prepared to deny her. That of course, rarely happened, because I would usually feel angry for a couple days or so, and then would revert to my usual self, and I would be ready for sex whenever the opportunity presented itself.

A number of years ago, we set up a code of sorts so that when one of us was interested in a sexual encounter, we would light a candle somewhere in the house, usually in our bedroom, but sometimes other places as well. Since we both love candles, this became a non-verbal indicator to each other what we were thinking. It gave Debby the time she needed and allowed us to be spontaneous at the same time. You better believe I always have a large supply of candles on hand!

Make Sex and Intimacy a High Priority in Your Marriage

One thing that we are constantly reminded of in our own marriage is the correlation between our relationship and our intimacy. You see, the closer our relationship, the more frequent the intimacy. Many people think it is the other way around—the more sex you have, the closer your relationship will be. This is not the case at all. As we often say, sex is a thermometer of your relationship, it is not the thermostat. Frequent sex will not ensure a close relationship, but a close relationship will most often produce a high level of intimacy and passion.

In our marriage, we place a high value on communication and expectations. When we talk things through, communicate our expectations, and then meet the expectations of one another, we are building up our relationship. Cultivating our relationship has a direct and usually immediate impact on the fruit of our relationship.

Guys, it's pretty clear. Value your bride, and she will respond in kind. She will want to fulfill your desires. She will want to ensure your sexual gratification. If she sees you putting her needs first, it is a natural desire of hers to meet your needs. That way, you both win.

What do you think of when you read the words "value your bride?" Think about something of yours that you value. There is a television commercial running right now for an insurance company and they ask what you would put up on a pedestal. In other words, what's valuable to you? For some, it may be a car, or a collection, maybe an award or a trophy you have earned.

When you value that item, what do you do to it or with it? Most likely you protect it from damage. You keep it in a special place and ensure no harm comes to it. Maybe you handle it with care when you move it, when you use it, or when you show it off. It's a similar mindset with your wife. When you value her, you protect her. You ensure no harm comes to her. You respect her, you are sensitive to her, and you try to understand her. Throughout the day, it's the small acts of kindness that make a difference and demonstrate your love for her.

> ...sex is a thermometer of your relationship, it is not the thermostat.

When you have something of value, you protect it at all cost. That's what a man needs to do for his wife. When she hurts, comfort her. Hold her and reassure her that you are there for her. When we value someone, we need to be fully absorbed in caring for that person and be willing to do whatever it takes, at all costs. When we truly value our spouse, we will love unconditionally.

The same goes for the women as well. Value your husband, which means care for, treasure, and unconditionally love and protect your man. When we do this for each other, the relationship grows stronger and produces much fruit.

Here's my disclaimer . . . it must be genuine. Remember guys, she's reading this book, too! If, as the guys at the office may say, "you wanna get lucky tonight" and you try to sugar-coat things you say, you try too hard in a superficial way to do things and you are not sincere, this will backfire on you and you will get burned. She will see through your empty gestures, she will know your intentions are selfish and you will be blowing out that candle tonight with a frustrated sigh. Your wife knows you well enough to know when you are genuine and when you are putting on a show just to get what you want.

~

In your sexual relationship, it is crucial that you establish mutual boundaries; it's important that you communicate what those boundaries should be, and then you respect those boundaries. Trying new things and being creative in your sexual relationship is good and is an important part of keeping your relationship fresh, but be sure to understand where the limits are, and ensure that your wife (or husband) is comfortable with that creativity. Romance and intimacy was intended for us to fully enjoy one another within the bonds of marriage, but there may be personal preferences that one or both of you have that may limit some of that creative thinking.

Creativity is healthy and has the potential to add fuel to the fire of our passion, but when new ideas or untested sexual positions are outside of the comfort zone, it is important to be open to each other's feelings. If you aren't comfortable talking about your sexual relationship, make that a goal of yours. Start with something easy, such as a favorite memory or your favorite romantic setting, and build on your comfort level from there.

It is important to be able to openly discuss what you like and what you don't like when it comes to your sexual relationship. Together you should be able to talk about how you can fulfill each other's desires. Don't be shy; the intimacy that is shared by the two of you is unique and unparalleled. It is a connection that cannot be made with anyone else. The more open you are in talking about your sexual needs and desires, the more you will both be able to satisfy one another. This is certainly not a topic or area that you should avoid talking about; rather, it is another area of your relationship where it is critical that you discuss what you both want, need, and expect.

It is important, men, to take care of your wife's needs and don't allow sex to become a self-gratifying exercise. We need to take the time to ensure that our wife enjoys sex as much as we do, and we need to be sensitive to what gives her pleasure. Of course, keeping in mind the law of reciprocity, the more we focus on meeting her needs, the more our own needs are met. When you take the time to set the mood, such as lighting candles or putting on soft music, and you focus on fulfilling her needs, she will be more open and responsive to you than on the days when that level of preparation and romance aren't possible.

For us, we have always maintained the privacy of our bedroom. Besides being a place of rest, our bedroom is where we share our most intimate moments, and it is exclusively for us. We don't allow the kids to sleep in our bed with us (except maybe during an extreme thunder and lightning storm!), and we decorate our room with romantic pictures of the two of us together. It is amazing what you can do to transform your walls and windows on a tight budget to create an atmosphere of love and romance. Sheer curtains, pictures of the two of you holding hands on the beach (or your favorite place), and big fluffy pillows are the bare necessities. And of course, we have candles everywhere.

There was a particular house we lived in a few years ago that was pretty small and out of necessity we had our computer in our bedroom. We were a family of six living in a 1,234 square-foot house, with one bathroom. The bathroom caused numerous challenges along the way, but that's another story! We were so happy when we were able to move the computer and home office out of our bedroom, and we encourage you to do the same. Don't allow your bedroom to become the gathering place for family, the home office, or the craft and hobby room. It should be your special space, exclusively set apart for the two of you.

Ladies, as much as they may not admit it, men do value romance and intimacy, not just sex. It may seem that they are only interested in one thing, but women need to realize that men are just created differently. They are visually stimulated much quicker than women, and they don't need much advance notice, but they do appreciate a romantic evening just as women do.

One way a woman can demonstrate love for her husband is to take care of herself and the way she looks. Too many times when marriages are in crisis and the couples are in the throes of divorce, one or both of the spouses decide that it's time to go to the gym and get into shape. They begin to care more about what they look like because they are or soon will be "back on the market."

We challenge you to do that now while you are married! Why not take better care of yourself for your spouse? Once you begin this journey of being the best you can be for your spouse, the feeling will be contagious and your spouse will most likely respond by doing the same. Why wait until you are on the market again? Why not choose to stay off the market and get in shape for your spouse? Your husband (or wife) will appreciate the extra time you take to present yourself in an appealing way, and you will feel good doing it.

In fact, your spouse totally deserves you to be at your very best! We all should do everything we can to be as attractive and desirable as possible

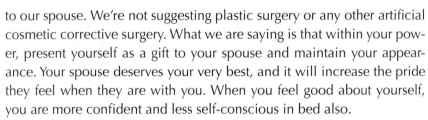

to our spouse. We're not suggesting plastic surgery or any other artificial cosmetic corrective surgery. What we are saying is that within your power, present yourself as a gift to your spouse and maintain your appearance. Your spouse deserves your very best, and it will increase the pride they feel when they are with you. When you feel good about yourself, you are more confident and less self-conscious in bed also.

[Debby] I absolutely love to go clothes shopping. I typically don't spend much money on myself, as our four kids are always in need of something, but when I do buy my clothes, I usually pick up several outfits and surprise Jason when he gets home from work.

The best part of my shopping is that I love to shop at Goodwill. There are some pretty affluent neighborhoods near my favorite Goodwill store and I can always find top name-brand clothes that are practically new, for a fraction of the retail price. By doing this, I can look nice for my husband and do so at a very low cost. I usually don't pay more than fifteen dollars for an outfit, which may have cost close to one hundred dollars when new.

Take a look at your wardrobe. Do you dress frumpy or are you fashionable? It makes a big difference. Style your hair, buy a new outfit once in a while (at your local second-hand store), and take care of your body. You will feel better about yourself and your husband will appreciate your efforts.

Ladies, it is vital that you look your best for your husband and that you do not let yourself go. I don't mean being uncomfortable all the time in fancy clothes, but dress in the latest styles. Be clean and presentable. Do your hair and make-up (if you typically wear make-up). Strive to be a woman your husband would be proud to show off to his friends.

Keep in mind, however, that just as you are attractive to your husband and you take the steps necessary to take care of yourself, you are bound to draw attention from other men at some point throughout your day. Remember that men are much more visually stimulated than women are, so be prepared to deal with this attention appropriately and always remember that your husband is your only priority. Do not deviate from the goal of building an amazing marriage and be sure to focus all of your attention on your husband.

This extreme make-over, to borrow a popular phrase, doesn't need to cost you hundreds of dollars. When I buy my clothes at Goodwill, I am very selective and pick only name brand items that are like new. I am able to add name brand items to my wardrobe on a regular basis without stretching our family budget. My friends are continually amazed when I reveal the fact that most of my outfits are from a second-hand shop.

Sweatshirts and pajama bottoms certainly have their place in my wardrobe, but these items are not what I wear to impress my husband. First and foremost, you should be concerned with looking your very best for your husband, specifically when you are both out in public.

Men, this idea is for you, too. I usually buy Jason's clothes as well, so when I see a really great looking man I make a mental note of what he is wearing and make purchases for my husband accordingly. He's not as fond of buying his clothes at Goodwill as I am, but I watch for clearance sales and am pretty selective with his clothes, too.

For a reasonable cost, we both look great for each other and feel good being together in public. One of Jason's friends recently told him that he is embarrassed to walk through the mall with his wife because of how she takes care for herself. Don't allow this to happen in your relationship. How you present yourself to your spouse has a direct impact on how he or she treats and respects you.

Satisfy Your Spouse's Needs on a Regular and Consistent Basis

When we talk about satisfying the needs of your spouse, we are not only referring to sexual needs. Remember, sex is a thermometer, not a thermostat. You can't set the temperature of your relationship by meeting one another's sexual desires. You set the temperature of your relationship by placing his or her needs before your own. You take responsibility for things around the house and you pitch in to help with the various details of running the household. There are many needs that must be met before your sexual needs can be met on a consistent basis.

If we took a survey and asked how frequently people thought *their spouse* wanted to have sex, the guys would most likely say once or twice a month and the ladies would probably say four to five days a week . . . or more. That's the difference in how men and women are wired. It's important to understand that difference and to have a better understanding of your spouse's needs.

We highly encourage you to cultivate your relationship and enjoy each other sexually on a frequent and regular basis. We obviously can't say what that frequency would look like for you, as each couple may be different. There may be health issues that need to be considered, among other mitigating circumstances and factors. One thing we do know is that if your health allows for sexual intercourse on a regular basis, the frequency of your sex is a great indicator (thermometer) of your relationship.

I (Jason) remember as a teenager, and most of you men can identify with this, thinking that I couldn't wait to get married because then I could have sex every day. While that may be the wishful thinking of every teenage boy, we all know it is vastly different from the reality of marriage. We highly doubt that your frequency will be every day, but do be sure to carve out time on a consistent basis just for the sheer pleasure of, well, pleasure.

Choosing to Make Your Sex Life Amazing

So how do you keep romance fresh and exciting and how do you have amazing sex? One effective way is through small impulsive gifts or notes. Random reminders of your love that you give to your lover. There are countless ways to demonstrate your love and keep your romance fresh, and you can do this on a budget.

Several years ago I wrote Debby a love note and mailed it to her. In that letter I described what our next date night would look like. I wrote of how I would arrange for the kids to be gone for the evening, how I would set out as many candles as possible throughout the house, and what I would prepare for dinner. I went on to describe the music we would be listening to, and scripted out a quiet evening alone. That gave her something to look forward to for a few days. If you've never done anything like that, give it a try. The fact that it came through the mail added suspense and intrigue.

When you do this, it is very important that you follow through on the date night, and if any unforeseen circumstances cause you to change to a different night than you had planned, be sure to follow through and reschedule as soon as possible. You need to continue to build trust and invest in your wife and in your relationship, and cancelled date nights may take a serious toll on your credibility.

Recently, I was working in Tacoma, Washington, which is approximately twenty miles from our home. About midday, one of my co-workers came to me and said that there was something on my car. Not knowing what he was referring to initially, I went out to the parking lot to see if someone banged their door into my car, or spilled garbage on the hood, or something like that.

I was pleasantly surprised to see, across the parking lot, a single red rose and what appeared to be a card. I went to my car to retrieve these gifts, and as I was returning to the building, the entire staff was waiting near the front door, undoubtedly anxious to see who it was from. Does the boss have a mistress? A girlfriend? A secret admirer?

They all know I am married but, unfortunately, there's a sense of intrigue and romance associated with a secret admirer or a secret lover. They all wanted to know who the rose was from. As I think about that, it was really pretty sad that they thought it may be from anyone other than my wife.

When I re-entered the building and saw them all standing there anxiously awaiting the juicy details, I was quick to credit my wife and let them know what a wonderful surprise it was for her to go so far out of her way to tell me that she loves me. Fortunately, I had talked to my wife a few hours earlier in the day and mentioned where I was, because she told me later that night that she thought I was in Issaquah, which is twenty-five miles in the opposite direction! She would have driven many miles in the wrong direction to leave a rose, and I wouldn't have been there. Again, solid communication is very important in any relationship.

As we have mentioned already, small gifts left in odd places, "I love you" notes, and other reminders of your love for each other are great ways to keep your romance fresh. Everyone would love to be recognized and receive a small token of love or appreciation, and if it is done in a public venue, it is even more precious. We know of one couple who mounted a dry erase board in their kitchen to leave notes for one another on the board every day.

Be creative. Go to your local dollar store, buy a dozen helium balloons and stuff her car with them while she is at the grocery store or at work. Hide a chocolate bar in the freezer with a note wrapped around it. Place a sticky note inside the sports page of the newspaper before he gets home. Bury a Hershey Kiss in the coffee grounds. There are hundreds of ideas, and the best part is, most won't break your budget.

One of the keys to unlocking romance in your marriage, and we've touched on it already, is valuing your spouse. We recently returned from an eleven-day vacation, and as I was backing into our driveway Debby

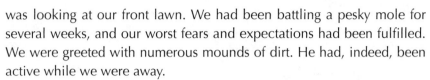

was looking at our front lawn. We had been battling a pesky mole for several weeks, and our worst fears and expectations had been fulfilled. We were greeted with numerous mounds of dirt. He had, indeed, been active while we were away.

As bad as the sight of our pock-marked lawn was, what drew her immediate attention was the gaping hole in the ground in the front corner of her garden by the road, where her prized lily had been. It was gone— ripped from the ground with a trail of dirt across the sidewalk. "Where's my lily?" she nearly screamed.

Someone had stolen the lily that she had planted five years prior when we first moved into the house. Whether it was someone who thought they needed her lily more than we did and helped themselves to it, or the work of pranksters, we may never know. What I realized right then and there was through this act of vandalism there was an opportunity for me to value my wife.

I printed up a mini-poster on our computer that offered a "$50 Reward for the return of the lily that was stolen from this spot last week" and attached it to a ground stake in the very corner of her garden where the lily was mercilessly snatched. I left it up for a week, to let the neighborhood know that we didn't appreciate the random act of selfish vandalism.

We never did recover the lily, but I was able to demonstrate to my wife my concern over her loss and a willingness to do whatever I could to rectify the situation. She turned down my offer to buy a replacement lily, so we now have purple flowers of some unknown species occupying the sacred ground where her lily once stood tall. It may or may not have been a successful recovery attempt, but perhaps just the thought and effort on my part sent her a message that I valued her and was sorry for her loss. Sometimes it's the little things in our marriage that make a big difference.

When you choose on a daily basis to value, honor, and respect your spouse, putting them first and seeing to it that their needs are met before yours, you won't need to worry about getting your own needs fulfilled. Remember the law of reciprocity. When I focus all my thoughts and energy on seeing to it that her needs are met, I don't have to worry about my own needs. She makes it a priority to meet my needs first just as I put her needs first.

Whether you have been married for a year or twenty years or more, don't allow sex to become a routine or predictable aspect of your life.

Rather, vary the timing, the location, the amount of fore-play and as much as possible we encourage you to be spontaneous. Take advantage of situations as they present themselves to spend a few moments alone. Whether you can take full advantage of a few quiet moments for intercourse or just for some light intimacy, these unexpected moments can be very meaningful to your relationship.

In addition to spontaneity, be intentional in your planning and make time on a consistent basis to do something special for yourselves. With just a little pre-planning and thoughtfulness, you can set up a romantic encounter that will add spice and intrigue to your relationship. This also allows you to vary your routines and to add spark to your relationship.

For one of our anniversaries, I arranged for our kids to spend the weekend with friends and booked a suite in a local hotel, with their romance package. The package included breakfast, a bottle of champagne, and a special box of chocolates. Because the hotel was local, we were close enough to home in the event of an emergency with our kids, yet we were able to enjoy a terrific weekend away with just the two of us.

There was another benefit of the hotel being local. After getting off work, I stopped at the hotel and checked in prior to going home. I had first stopped at the local dollar store and picked up some confetti and strands of red and silver foil, and spread that over the floor and the bed. I picked up a dozen roses and pulled the petals off ten of the roses and spread them out on the floor, making a trail from the door to the bedroom. The other two roses went in a vase on the dresser, one for each of us.

I lit a couple of large candles, and then went home to pick her up (looking back, this was not a smart move and is NOT recommended! Light those candles later when you both get to the hotel! Maybe you can come up with an excuse to run back to the car to retrieve something, and go to the room to light the candles before you both go to your room. Be creative, you'll find a way!)

When Debby and I arrived at the hotel, I left her in the car and went in to the lobby to "check in" (although I had already done so). I enjoyed a quick cup of coffee while simulating the check-in process, and then went out to get her and our luggage.

Her surprise as we entered the room and she saw the rose petals, the confetti, the chocolates, and candles was definitely worth the effort! We were able to enjoy the evening at our own pace, without being rushed due to the needs of our four kids. It was a special weekend that we will not soon forget!

On another occasion, I don't recall where our kids were but I do remember that we had the evening to ourselves. Debby was out running an errand and I ran a hot bath with bath oils for her and set up approximately fifty small votive candles, making a path of candles from the front door to the bathroom. With love songs playing softly in the background, I was able to create an intimate and romantic setting that was different from the norm. The hot bath was soothing and helped her to relax and forget the events of the day, if only for a few moments.

Ladies, occasionally, when your man comes home from work, slip into some lingerie and meet him at the door with a passionate kiss. Arrange for the kids to be out for the evening, or for a few hours, and let your imagination run wild. He's probably been secretly wishing you'd do that sometime!

A little creativity and thought goes a long way in keeping your romance fresh. Candles, lingerie, a romantic dinner for two on the back deck; there are countless ideas for you to choose from. If you have kids and know other couples that have kids, set up an arrangement with them so you trade off babysitting for date nights. It is important for you to have time alone, on a frequent basis, to keep your relationship strong and thriving.

Is It Ever Appropriate to Hold Out On Your Spouse?

One of the primary reasons for marriage is the sexual aspect. Marriage was designed for two people to enjoy each other sexually within the bonds and boundaries of a marriage covenant. Because of the "one man and one woman" nature of marriage and our commitment to be faithful to each other, we should not deny one another sexual pleasure. Otherwise, this denial of sexual intimacy may develop into a pattern, which could cause division in a marriage.

Now, this doesn't mean that we should expect the "fruits" of our marriage during disagreements and fights. It is natural to not want to have any intimate physical contact when there is a deep-seated argument or a disagreement. However, once your fellowship has been restored and forgiveness granted, celebrate it in bed! The longer one partner "holds out" and uses sex to teach the other a lesson or to get a point across, the harder it may be to work through the initial problem, as the lack of a physical relationship will add another dimension to the initial problem and perhaps prolong restoration.

We have been discussing marriage relationships with several couples and are shocked to hear that some of them have gone months without having sex. I often think of my friend Richard who usually can count on one hand the number of times he and his wife have had sex in the span of a year. I truly feel sorry for him! It is not healthy for a couple to refrain from sexual activity for a long period of time, unless there are physical limitations or health risks. When this happens, disagreements are magnified and additional conflict can materialize.

In most marriages, it is quite common for one spouse to desire to have sex on a particular day or night when it is the farthest thing from the mind of their spouse. With all the various pressures on us throughout the day, chances are great that one of you may want to initiate spontaneous love-making on exactly the wrong day or time. We have found that, along with many other aspects of our marriage, this is one subject where good communication is vitally important.

If I don't pick up on the nonverbal messages that Debby is sending throughout the evening that she is "not in the mood" and I try to initiate sex, she will sometimes tell me that the time is just not right. She's open and honest with me, without giving the famous "headache" excuse. Sometimes she gives me the reasons, and other times she doesn't.

There are times when I need to accept this and honor her wishes, yet there are also times when she understands that I have physical needs that must be met, and we have sex. It's important to realize that at different times, we both need to sacrifice for our spouse. When we are focused on putting each other first, we both win. The key is communicating your expectations and your needs, and coming to an understanding.

Biblical Perspective

The Bible has plenty to say about sex and the marriage relationship, and it isn't all negative warnings about fornication and adultery. In fact, read these words from the Song of Solomon, chapter 4:9–15:

"You have ravished my heart, my treasure, my bride. I am overcome by one glance of your eyes, by a single bead of your necklace. How sweet is your love, my treasure, my bride! How much better it is than wine! Your perfume is more fragrant than the richest of spices. Your lips, my bride, are as sweet as honey. Yes, honey and cream are under your tongue. The scent of your clothing is like that of the mountains and the cedars of Lebanon. You are like a private garden, my treasure, my bride!

You are like a spring that no one else can drink from, a fountain of my own. You are like a lovely orchard bearing precious fruit, with the rarest of perfumes: nard and saffron, calamus and cinnamon,

> God created sex and desires that the covenant of marriage will be a lifelong commitment

myrrh and aloes, perfume from every incense tree, and every other lovely spice. You are a garden fountain, a well of living water, as refreshing as the streams from the Lebanon mountains."

Furthermore, Song of Solomon 7:11–12 says, "Come, my love, let us go out to the fields and spend the night among the wildflowers. Let us get up early and go to the vineyards to see if the grapevines have budded, if the blossoms have opened, and if the pomegranates have bloomed. There I will give you my love." Sounds like a romance novel, doesn't it? There are many more verses on romance similar to these in Song of Solomon. Spend an evening reading this book of the Bible with your lover.

God created sex and desires that the covenant of marriage will be a lifelong commitment. Genesis 2:18 says, "Then the LORD God said, 'It is not good for the man to be alone. I will make a helper who is just right for him.'" As the Scriptures say, "A man leaves his father and mother and is joined to his wife, and the two are united into one" (Ephesians 5:31). Matthew 19:6 reads, "Since they are no longer two but one, let no one split apart what God has joined together."

God expects us to remain faithful to our spouse, and clearly indicates His judgment on those who practice immorality. "Give honor to marriage, and remain faithful to one another in marriage. God will surely judge people who are immoral and those who commit adultery" (Hebrews 13: 4). 1 Thessalonians 4:2–3 says, "For you remember what we taught you by the authority of the Lord Jesus. God's will is for you to be holy, so stay away from all sexual sin."

We encourage you as husband and wife to fully enjoy your sexual relationship. You are free to enjoy each other's sexuality and the pleasure you can bring to one another. While it is true that God designed sex and intended it for our pleasure, some may wonder if we as believers have the freedom to have sexual fantasies. Playful experimentation with one another and creativity is wholesome and can add variety to your sexual relationship, but we are cautioned to live a disciplined life and to control our thoughts. "Cast down arguments and every high thing that exalts itself against the knowledge of God, bringing every thought into captivity to the obedience of Christ" (2 Cor. 10:5).

According to 2 Timothy 2:22, "Run from anything that stimulates youthful lust." If your thoughts and fantasies include anything that takes your attention and desires away from your spouse, you cross the line of what is acceptable to God. Ephesians 5:3 says "Let there be no sexual immorality, impurity, or greed among you. Such sins have no place among God's people." If you fantasize about a particular romantic getaway or adventure and this fantasy only involves you and your spouse, you have the freedom to indulge and enjoy the fantasy.

As we have indicated, it is never appropriate to hold out on one another as a form of punishment or depriving one another of pleasure. Doing so could cause one or the other of you to lose self-control and fall into an adulterous relationship. We read in 1 Corinthians 7:2–5, "But because there is so much sexual immorality, each man should have his own wife, and each woman should have her own husband. The husband should fulfill his wife's sexual needs, and the wife should fulfill her husband's needs. The wife gives authority over her body to her husband, and the husband gives authority over his body to his wife. Do not deprive each other of sexual relations, unless you both agree to refrain from sexual intimacy for a limited time so you can give yourselves more completely to prayer. Afterward, you should come together again so that Satan won't be able to tempt you because of your lack of self-control."

Plan a romantic getaway for you and your spouse, and indulge in one another. Stoke the flames of your passion and renew the freshness in your relationship.

Chapter 4

One Day At a Time

"You will come to know that what appears today to be a sacrifice will prove instead to be the greatest investment that you will ever make."

~ *Gorden B. Hinkley*

One night last year Debby and I were having a discussion with our kids about attitudes and respect. It had been a particularly tough day with the kids arguing most of the day, and one of our daughters always feels the need to be right and get the last word in. She can't stand being wrong, and must always have a word to say in response to others. We continually encourage our children to choose their own attitudes, regardless of whether other people around them choose good attitudes or not, and we were discussing what had transpired that day. That particular night, she said she didn't think choosing her own attitude can happen that easily. Her emotions were stretched too far and she just couldn't get a handle on her attitude.

I told her that she needs to be persistent, as it won't happen right away. It often takes time to separate oneself from a hostile or emotional situation and choose to change an attitude. She's right, it is difficult to change an attitude, but I encouraged her to stay with it and to be persistent. I went on to tell her that she has to make an effort each and every day to choose proper attitudes and she will see a difference; one day at a time she will find that it gets easier and easier to make these choices.

It had been a cold week and as we were having this discussion we still had snow on the ground from the previous night. This was somewhat unusual, as it typically doesn't snow in Seattle, and when it does, it rarely stays around for longer than twenty-four hours.

As we were discussing attitudes and the persistence required to choose our attitudes wisely, I looked outside and saw that it was gently snowing again. I suddenly blurted out, "You know, it takes a lot of snowflakes to make a snowman."

You can imagine the family's surprise with that seemingly unrelated statement coming from me. "Listen," I said, "you've all watched our weather. When it rains and the rain begins to turn to snow, it doesn't accumulate right away. The snowflakes hit the wet ground and they melt. Over time, the ground begins to get slushy and then the snow begins to accumulate. It's a long process and it takes a consistent snowfall to build up the accumulation. Therefore, it takes a lot of snowflakes to make a snowman!"

She still thought I was crazy, but I went on to explain that it takes repeated efforts on her part to change her attitude, which in turn will change the attitudes of others around her. Whether their attitudes change or not, she is only responsible for her own attitude. That's all she can control. We wanted her to learn that, with a repeated and consistent effort, she can begin to influence others around her in a positive manner.

This same principle applies to married couples, employee/employer relationships, or any other relationship you have with people. You can only determine your own attitude, but that attitude can have a significant impact on people around you. It's important to surround yourself with positive people, as they also have an impact on you and your attitude.

To have a truly amazing marriage, there is work that must be done every day, without fail. From the moment you wake up in the morning to the moment you pillow your head at night, there are choices that must be made. Building value in your spouse, putting your spouse's needs before your own, respecting your spouse more than others, and building trust in each other should be lifelong goals, but they also need to be part of your daily routine. It's the little choices we make each and every day that determine the quality of our relationships.

Make a conscious decision every day to love your spouse and make it a point to tell your spouse each day that you love them, both verbally and otherwise. This could be a love note left where they will find it, a phone call during the day, or some other creative method of expressing your love. Mix it up and avoid repetition. Regardless of how you choose to communicate your love for one another, include verbal affirmation frequently. We believe this is extremely important to build and maintain a strong relationship. This one element, when done consistently, can work wonders in taking your marriage to a heightened level of intimacy, communication, and strength. So many children, all over the world are being brought up in households where they have never heard their father tell their mother that he loves her. What a tragedy!

If you make the decision every day to show your spouse love in such a

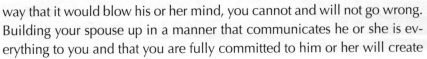

way that it would blow his or her mind, you cannot and will not go wrong. Building your spouse up in a manner that communicates he or she is everything to you and that you are fully committed to him or her will create in your spouse a desire to do the same for you. The well-known saying, "What goes around comes around" rings true in marriages as well!

> Kids need to see their parents, specifically their father, demonstrate love through actions

There is nothing "macho" about refusing to show emotions! As a matter of fact, it can build up walls and ultimately destroy your marriage. This could be a direct result of control and pride, which are two big issues that have the potential to destroy marriages. Oftentimes men feel the need to control the situation they are facing and manipulate the circumstances for their gain. We men can also be extremely prideful, refusing to allow our true emotions to surface. Take note of this next statement—real men cry and real men tell their wives that they love them. It doesn't make you a bigger man if you suppress your emotions and refuse to allow yourself to openly express how you feel. If you've never had this type of emotion modeled for you, break the cycle and model it for your kids. What makes you a man of great reputation and high regard is being in a lifelong marriage that is remarkable, and that others can see it as being truly different and unique.

Kids need to see their parents, specifically their father, demonstrate love through actions and physical touch. Of course, as far as the physical touch goes, practice this concept within reasonable limits and boundaries. We make certain that we tell each other on a daily basis "I love you" and we frequently kiss in front of our kids. Now, we do keep the long and passionate kisses out of their sight, of course, but we feel it is important to demonstrate our love for each other on a daily basis, and our kids need to see that in our lives. Recently a friend of our teenage daughters told them that he has never seen his parents kiss. That's a sad testament to his family life.

Recently we attended the Gymnastics Tour of Champions, which featured the 2008 Olympians. We were fortunate to get there early enough to participate in a Q&A time with a few of the athletes before the exhibition, and we heard the athletes talk about their training routines. One of the gymnasts told us that he has been training since he was five years old. It has taken him many years of training and preparation for the opportunity to compete in the Olympics. Athletes in every sport have a rigid training routine each day to get in shape and to stay in a competitive condition.

In our marriages, we need to have that same type of diligence. It takes hard work, dedication, and diligence to make the sacred covenant of marriage work. If you truly want your marriage to be amazing, you need to discipline yourself daily, in a similar manner as these Olympians. Just as an athlete cannot qualify to compete at the Olympic level without a disciplined training routine, we cannot expect to be successful in our marriage relationship without a disciplined routine.

Consider our military. The men and women in our armed forces train the same skill over and over and over again, until they can perform the task to perfection. I recall my time in the Army Basic Training when we would break down and reassemble our Colt 1911 .45 caliber semi-automatic pistol until we could do it with a blindfold on. It's the routines and discipline, practiced relentlessly, that allow our soldiers, sailors, and airmen and women to respond correctly in a high-stress environment, where their response to a problem or incident may have life or death consequences.

Our relationship needs the same amount of dedication and consistency. We cannot honor, value, and respect our spouse a few days a week and then be self-absorbed for the remainder of the week, and expect our relationship to be solid. We can't treat our spouse in a loving and respectful manner for a day or two when we think it may benefit us, and then turn around and be arrogant and selfish the other five days of the week and expect our spouse to have the desire to be loving and intimate. It just doesn't work that way. We must do these things on a consistent basis, one day at a time, each and every day. This is how we build trust, so that when we encounter troubled waters we can navigate through and around the storm and come out on the other side with our relationship not only intact but stronger than when we first faced the storm.

There are so many different challenges married couples face on a daily basis, and when we make it a habit to do the right things and focus on our relationship, we are in a much stronger position to fight off the various forms of attack on our relationship. Is our relationship perfect? Of course not. We struggle with many of the same things that you are struggling with. The difference in an amazing marriage and a struggling marriage is how you deal with those challenges. Don't allow minor issues to become major battles and always deal with your struggles head on.

We have learned over the years how to communicate with each other and how to express what we are feeling, regardless of what we think the other may say or feel about that. We have learned to be real and honest with one another as we work through adversity. It isn't always easy, and we have many battle scars from the times we have failed, but we persevere and make a daily effort to improve. Focusing on yourself and using statements like, "I feel," goes a long way in helping your spouse to understand your feelings without them feeling as if they are being attacked.

Biblical Perspective

Thank God sincerely and genuinely every day for your spouse. In addition to thanking God for your spouse, show your spouse in a tangible and demonstrative way that you are thankful for them. Remember Proverbs 18:22; our wives are valuable enough for God to refer to them as a treasure. Every man should treat his wife as a valuable treasure.

Don't simply thank God for your spouse on a daily basis; pray for them. Pray that He will strengthen the bond between you and that your love for each other will grow stronger. Pray for opportunities each day to demonstrate your love to your spouse. Remember, God is the third strand in your marriage (Ecclesiastes 4:9–12) and He desires to help you grow and strengthen your relationship. Men, when you pray for your wife on a daily basis, she will not only be grateful for that, she will also feel more confident in your spiritual leadership. She will know that you are continually lifting her up to God and she will see in you a sincere desire to follow Christ and to seek His guidance. Women, when you keep your husband in your prayers, he will be encouraged that you are seeking God's direction in your relationship.

It's a well-known fact; life constantly throws the unexpected our way. If we are not grounded in our faith when Satan strikes, we will be more vulnerable to his attack and we may falter. We are constantly battered by the allure of the world and we need to be grounded in His word; we need to be renewed day by day. (2 Cor. 4:8–9, 16)

Paul prayed for the mighty inner strength of the Holy Spirit, in Ephesians 3:16. If we do that, He will respond and give us the peace that enables us to overcome the trials or problems we face. I love 1 John

4:4b, which says, "Greater is He that is in you than he that is in the world." (KJV) If we rely solely on Jesus Christ for our inner strength, He will give us what we need to overcome! His desire is for you and me to be victorious.

Let's face it, most of you reading this book have some degree of turmoil in your life and perhaps even in your marriage. We are highly encouraged that you picked up our book and have a desire to improve your relationship. If you are a Christian, one of the keys to discovering your amazing marriage is the peace of God. This is truly the heartbeat of an amazing marriage that is centered on Christ.

> Once you have peace with God, you can have the peace of God.

John 14:27 tells us this about the peace of God: "Peace I leave with you; my peace I give you. I do not give to you as the world gives. Do not let your hearts be troubled and do not be afraid." (NIV) He gives us His peace and His desire is that we live without fear.

You see, the world says that peace is the absence of turmoil, but the truth of the matter is that for Christians, peace is the presence of God in the midst of turmoil. With God, you can have peace in your marriage in the midst of whatever turmoil you are enduring. He promises to give you peace sufficient for your needs at the time. We do not need to be fearful and we can have assurance that God is in control of our situation.

Have you turned to Him in the midst of your turmoil? Have you given your problems to God? Cast all your cares and troubles upon Him and leave your baggage at the foot of the cross. He can give you peace and sufficient strength to overcome and prevail, even when defeat seems inevitable. Let not your hearts be troubled, He will give you a peace that surpasses all understanding (Philippians 4:7) and that will enable you to endure the hardships you face on a daily basis.

Once you have peace with God, you can have the peace of God. This means that even though there may be difficult times and turmoil in your relationship, and that is the case with every relationship from time to time, you can have the peace of God and know that you will see better days. If you don't have a personal relationship with God, make that a priority.

In the words of the late Ronald Reagan, "our best days are yet to come." If we continue to grow in our relationship with the Lord and with each other, our love grows deeper, stronger, and more resilient to the pressures of the world. It's like how a callous builds up and makes the skin more resistant to blisters. When we renew ourselves day by day in the Word, we grow closer and closer to the Lord and we strengthen the bonds of our relationship. When we do this, we are more resistant to the temptations and the effects of sinful choices. By no means are we perfect and sinless, but a close relationship with the Lord helps us resist the temptations. James 4:7 clearly illustrates this point: "So humble yourselves before God. Resist the devil and he will flee from you."

According to 1 Corinthians 10:13, we have this assurance: "The temptations in your life are no different from what others experience. And God is faithful. He will not allow the temptation to be more than you can stand. When you are tempted, he will show you a way out so that you can endure." When we are walking in the Spirit and when we are in submission to God, we are more alert and aware of His leading and direction in our life and are more apt to follow the prompting of the Holy Spirit. God allows us to be tempted, as Christ was tempted in every way we are, but He protects us in that He will not allow any temptation to be greater than that which we can withstand.

The greatest asset we have in our relationship, and that you can have in yours, is a relationship with Christ. In part, the relationship we have with Christ is what makes us different and is what makes people ask us about our positive relationship. When you have Christ in your life, you are unique, you are different. You see life through a different perspective and your value system is different. We have incredible joy and peace in our relationship with one another because of our relationship with God.

This is not to say that non-Christians cannot have a successful and amazing marriage; of course they can. Christians and other faith-based couples don't have an exclusive hold on successful relationships. However, the relationship we as believers have with Christ impacts every other relationship we have. This is especially true of our most intimate relationship; the relationship we have with our spouse. We believe that we can experience both the love of God and the peace of God, with the example that Christ loved us to the death. This gives a whole new meaning to the vow, till death do us part.

We know that we are going to be faced with trials and challenging circumstances on a continual basis. However, as we meditate on His Word and renew our faith one day at a time, we can persevere and defeat the enemy wherever and whenever he shows up. We are children of the Most High God, and when we walk in faith on a daily basis, we are renewed and filled with His Spirit, which enables us to face our trials already knowing that we will be victorious. Remind yourself of this on a regular basis: I am a child of God; therefore, I can overcome and defeat the enemy.

Your faith, and what you believe, will influence every aspect of your life. As a believer, follow these five steps and you will see amazing results in your personal life and in your marriage:

1. **Ask God to reveal His plan and purpose for your life.** He put you on this earth to fulfill the destiny that He has designed for you. God wants you to fulfill that destiny, or His purpose. Jeremiah 29:11 says, "'For I know the plans I have for you,' says the LORD. 'They are plans for good and not for disaster, to give you a future and a hope.'" Psalm 138:8 says, "The Lord will work out his plans for my life—for your faithful love, O Lord, endures forever. Don't abandon me, for you made me." When you pray and ask God to reveal His purpose for your life, ask Him to reveal how you fit into His plans, not how He fits into your plans. We are His workmanship, created in Christ Jesus (Eph. 2:10), which God has ordained before the foundation of the world.

2. **Ask God to reveal what you need to give up or change in your life** to elevate and grow your marriage. You need to die to self; in other words, you need to get out of the way and allow God to work through your life. God will reveal to you areas that are sin (1 Cor. 4:3–5) and He will bring your darkest secrets to light. The Bible also tells us that we cannot serve two masters (Matt 6:24 and Luke 16:13). We need to die to self and turn from sin and "sell out" to God in order to be useful to the kingdom and fulfill the purpose He has for us.

3. **Follow God's direction**; do not deviate from His plans, even if you think you have a better plan. I find myself challenged with this as I often think that I have things all figured out. I may have a timeframe in my mind for something that doesn't come to pass, and I find myself asking God why He hasn't allowed it to happen, or why I am still waiting. There are many examples in my life where I look back over the span of a few years and realize that God's timing was perfect, but as I recall living through those years

I remember being anxious and wanting to see things happening at a faster pace. I frequently need a reminder that God has things under control and His timing is far better than mine could ever be. Philippians 4:6 says, "Do not be anxious about anything, but in everything, by prayer and petition, with thanksgiving, present your requests to God." (NIV)

4. **Men, be the man. Women, allow your man to be the man.** By this we mean take responsibility for your actions and for your family. Provide the spiritual leadership that your wife so desperately needs and "man up." God has called you to lead your family and to accept that responsibility (Eph. 5:22–30). We are also to love our wives unconditionally, to the point of giving up our life for her. We are to provide for the needs of our families (1 Timothy 5:8). Besides providing financially for your family, you are to model Christ for your wife and be proactive in helping to meet her spiritual needs.

5. **Put one another first in your life, in all things.** Outside of your relationship with God, your spouse should be your first priority. Consider activities in your life that fill your time and deprive you of quality time together. Eliminate some frivolous activities and give your spouse the time you are currently wasting away. Some of you may say that you can't possibly work anything else into your schedule; to that I challenge you to find the time.

Use a small notepad that you can carry with you throughout your day and write down all the time you spend in your various activities. This log should include time spent in getting ready for work, eating breakfast, commuting to work, your meal period at work, the commute home, time reading the paper, time checking your e-mail, time watching television or movies, etc. Do this for several days and then evaluate the results. You will see where you can eliminate certain activities, or shorten the time spent in some activities, to free up some time to spend with the one to whom you have pledged your eternal love and life. Making adjustments in your daily routine to give your time to your spouse is a gift he or she will treasure.

By doing these things, you demonstrate to your spouse that you love them and you are committed to investing in your relationship on a daily basis. When you are grounded in your faith and your trust is in the Lord, you will find His perfect peace—Isaiah 26:3 says, "You will keep in perfect peace him whose mind is steadfast, because he trusts in you." (NIV)

Chapter 5

Breaking the Cycle of Divorce

"The most important thing a father can do for his children is to love their mother." ~ Seneca

D ebby and I both grew up in families of divorce. I was around three or four years of age when my parents divorced and I have very few early childhood memories of my parents home together. For years, my mom raised my brother, two sisters, and I as a single parent and, to this day, I don't know how she did it. Throughout my childhood, we didn't have much, but what we did have was plenty. We never seemed to have an abundance, but there was always "enough." I find it interesting to note how your perspective of what constitutes enough changes as your circumstances change.

This would be a good time and place to say "thank you" to my mom, for all those years of struggling to feed us, clothe us, and put us through Christian school. I know my mom worked several jobs to make ends meet, and when those ends didn't or couldn't meet, well, somehow we managed to get along. Whether it was friends, relatives, or people from our church lending a hand, I never knew. Thanks Mom!

I never had the newest fashion designs. In fact, sometimes I didn't even have new clothes. Having an older brother, it was not uncommon to be the recipient of something "new," but it was really just new to me. The toys were often hand-me-downs and eating out was a luxury, but through my mom's daily sacrifices, she did what she could to provide. I learned a lot of great life lessons during those times, lessons that have stayed with me through the years that I am trying to pass on to my own kids, just under different circumstances.

Contentment is not based on whatever material possessions we own, but on who we love and who we surround ourselves with. It is a mind-set that we develop; a conscious decision to be happy or satisfied with who you are or what you have. While neither Debby nor I had much in the way of material possessions growing up, our families were content. In fact, both of our families were happy, because our relationships were strong. Relationships are far more important than money, possessions, and the accumulation of our stuff.

Simply put, divorce is not an option.

When I was about twelve or so, my mother met a man and married, only to end up in divorce court a year and a half later. Both of my parents remarried, and then both divorced. Both remarried yet again, and remain in those commitments as we write this. Debby's biological father was her mom's second marriage. They divorced when she was five, and both of her parents went on to marry again, and also remain in those commitments today.

We certainly don't wish to paint our parents in any bad light; we only mention this to make the point that divorce is a cycle, which often leads to yet another divorce. We must break that cycle and demonstrate to our children that divorce is not an option. The next generation needs to see the value of marriage compared to the potential disaster of divorce.

With both of us being raised in a broken home, we agreed early on that if we were to make the commitment of marriage to one another, it would be for life. We would live out the "till death do us part" commitment and we agreed that divorce is simply not an option. Long before I asked her to marry me at Lion's Field in Bremerton, Washington, we had a number of discussions on this topic. If we couldn't agree that above all else this was one foundation we would build our relationship on, we decided we should not marry. This was one of the commitments we made to one another that we would build our future upon. We have been through many fierce storms and could have taken the easy out that divorce offers, but we have weathered them all, growing stronger in the process.

Both of us had experienced divorce from the perspective of a child, and we have been committed since the very beginning of our marriage to break the cycle. I am the only child in my family who has not been divorced, and that is a constant reminder to me that Debby and I need to work daily to keep us (our covenant) a reality. Simply put, divorce is not an option. Even when we have the most fierce disagreement or fight and we cannot see eye to eye on an issue, we know that the end result will be that we are in this relationship forever, until death do us part, so we have to find a way for reconciliation.

Knowing that we will be forgiven if we are unfaithful or otherwise break trust with one another doesn't give us license to abuse the relationship, but it does give us comfort knowing that we are both committed to making this relationship work, regardless of the storms we encounter.

If divorce is an option that has not been removed from the equation in your relationship, it may be easier to eventually find yourself on the doorstep of divorce when you encounter life's most disastrous catastrophes. It may be easy to consider divorce as an option, even subconsciously, if you don't commit to one another and agree that divorce is completely out of the question.

Commit together, as soon as practically possible, and come to an agreement that divorce is not and will not be an option in your marriage. Period. Regardless of the circumstances or the problems you face, divorce cannot be considered. This mindset of having the ultimate goal reconciliation forces you to consider options you may not have thought about. This, of course, is assuming that it is physically safe for you to continue in your relationship. A lifelong commitment cannot ever be a "license" to do your own thing or betray your relationship.

Physical, emotional, and mental abuse can be present in a relationship and we would never encourage someone to stay in a relationship that would cause harm to you or your children. If you find yourself in an abusive relationship, we encourage you to get help from trained professionals. There are many different agencies and organizations to assist you. You do not have to face this abuse alone, and you certainly need to get yourself and your children to safety. If you are not sure where to begin, you can contact your local police department, the social services office in your community, or a local church or synagogue.

Recently we were vacationing in Tempe, Arizona, and as we were enjoying the sunshine and lounging in and around the pool at my Uncle Pete's house, Debby told him to ask me what project we were working on. Now, before I tell you his response, it has been interesting to hear the varied responses we get when we tell people we are writing a book on marriage. Most are supportive, though some friends and family look at us as if we are crazy, and there have been a few who have thought it presumptuous of us that we think we are well equipped to write such a book as this.

Uncle Pete's first response was, "Oh cool." But then he simply said, "Be careful writing a book on marriage." We didn't need him to explain, as we both instantly knew what he meant by that comment. We have been blessed to have been able to weather some horrible storms in our marriage, but we know we can't let our guard down, not even for an instant, and neither can you.

Just because we have put our thoughts and ideas on paper regarding our marriage, we know we need to be diligent and make daily decisions to love each other unconditionally to keep our marriage strong. Simply reading or writing a book will not be the difference maker. You can read our ideas and even put them into practice, but that alone will not guarantee your marriage will be amazing. It takes work to produce an amazing marriage—hard work and an uncommon commitment toward one another.

Uncle Pete went on to tell us of some friends of theirs who ended in divorce after attending a marriage conference. How tragic! I also know of a couple who attended a marriage conference here in Seattle, during which the husband revealed some things to his wife which ultimately lead to their divorce. Right there in the hotel room of the conference, rather than coming closer together they began the process of divorce!

Please don't think that a conference, a speaker, or a book will fix your problems and lead to eternal marital bliss. In fact, we believe that with the more knowledge you have and the more information you are privy to, the higher the level of responsibility and accountability you will be held to. It has been said that to whom much is given, much is required.

Quality Time Together

One important factor in marriage and your commitment to staying together is the quality of the time spent with one another. We encourage you to carve time out of your day to focus on your mate. Every situation will be different, so we can't tell you what would be right for you. Work schedules, school schedules, sports, activities, and other responsibilities on your time will dictate what is right for your particular situation.

The "when" is not the important part; it's the doing. Set aside time for your spouse. Just the two of you. For some, the mornings may work best. For others, it may be in the evening, perhaps the few quiet moments sitting and talking together after the kids are in bed. The important thing is that you set this time aside with consistency.

Quiet time together is an important aspect of a successful marriage and one that you will recognize the benefits of immediately. One thought on this before we go any further: the amount of time is not important. If all you can carve out in the beginning is five to ten minutes, start there. As you recognize the value of quality time together, you will start to see where you can steal a few minutes from a project or activity to give you more time together. Turn off the television, pry yourself away from the computer, avoid bringing your work home, and spend those found moments together. You will begin to see, almost immediately, the benefits of spending quality time together and you will begin to make this a higher priority in your marriage. As you do this, the benefits you reap will impact you and your spouse, as well as your kids, in a spectacular way.

For those moments when it is just the two of you, focus all of your energy and attention on your spouse. Ask them what they did today (or yesterday, if your time is in the morning). Find out what is going on in their life during the times that you are apart. Get him or her to open up and share their daily activities, so you can experience their day, too.

Share in your spouse's accomplishments, dreams, excitement, fears, and concerns. This is a time to let your spouse know that he or she is the most important person in the world. This is your spouse's time to confide in you and you can both plan your future together. This is time to laugh together, cry together, and dream together.

If, however, there is an absence of trust, there will naturally be an absence of communication as well. If there has been damage to the relationship, something that has strained the level of trust, perhaps infidelity or even suspected infidelity, this will be a very difficult step. We address this absence of trust in more detail in the chapter on forgiveness. We encourage you to read that chapter carefully, whether or not you have suffered a breach of trust in your relationship.

If you have not suffered a serious breach of trust, you are truly blessed, as trust can be broken in so many different ways. Continue to keep up your guard and stay keenly aware of outside influences that have the potential to shatter your relationship. Do not take the good times for granted, and work diligently to protect your marriage.

Are You a Statistic or a Success?

According to Jennifer Baker of the Forest Institute of Professional Psychology in Springfield, Missouri, 50 percent of first marriages, 67 percent of second, and 74 percent of third marriages end in divorce.[1] That is a staggering number, and if you are in your second, third, or even forth marriage, odds are heavily weighed against your making it. It is important that you know that, and make conscious decisions to break the cycle of divorce.

For those of you who have been through a divorce, don't look back, look forward. You may have been the victim in the marriage, or you may have been the one who caused the break-up. Either way, if you have remarried, you owe it to yourself and your current spouse to make the commitment of a lifetime to stay in your marriage. As we outlined, the statistics show that the divorce numbers are higher in multiple marriage relationships. In other words, the chances of ending your relationship in a divorce are much higher if you have previously been divorced.

Let not your heart be troubled! There is hope for you! You can break the cycle and make a commitment to your spouse to make this relationship last. You can't undo the past and you can't turn back the clock, but what you can do is focus on the present and the future.

According to Shelley Stile, a certified Divorce Recovery Life Coach, if you are divorced, it is important to forgive your ex-husband or ex-wife, as you need to break the emotional tie that you have with that person. She says, "Forgiveness is the ability to let go of blames, resentments, upsets, and negative emotions we hold against a particular person. We may have had a physical divorce but we are still tied to that person by a very taut rope. By remaining in blame, resentment, or hatred, we keep ourselves locked to the pain that we are trying to escape. We cannot move forward into a new life under these conditions."[2]

It is important to forgive your previous spouse, but you must focus all your attention and effort on making your current marriage permanent. You do not need to meet with an ex-spouse in a face-to-face meeting in order to forgive them; rather, you can forgive them and release them of the pain they caused you without seeing them. In the same article referenced above, Shelley Stile says, "Remember, there is no need to verbally forgive this person. You need not write them a letter or have an in-person forgiveness conversation. Forgiveness is something you do for yourself

---

1   The divorce rate in America for first marriage versus second or third marriage per Divorcerate.com

2   http://www.divinecaroline.com/22090/51990-forgive-divorce

and so if you write a letter, then save it or burn it. Forgiveness is an inner dialogue." You would not want to do anything that would jeopardize your current relationship and you certainly would not want to try and grant or seek forgiveness from a divorced spouse without the knowledge of your current spouse. This should not be done in secrecy but in absolute transparency.

If you are in a second marriage, we encourage you to view this marriage as your first, and your last. Don't allow a repeat of the pain and hurt that resulted from your divorce. Avoid making the mistakes that plagued your first marriage, and openly communicate any "red flags" that you may see with your spouse. Honest communication, above all else, is crucial to the success of your marriage.

"The institution of marriage is in serious trouble," said David Popenoe, report co-author and co-director of the National Marriage Project at Rutgers. "Americans are now less likely to marry than ever before, and those who do marry seem to be less happy than in previous decades. And despite a modest decline in the divorce rate, nearly 50 percent of all marriages are projected to end in divorce or permanent separation."[3]

In March 2008, the Barna Group issued marriage and divorce statistics and reported four in five people will be married at least once and one in three will be divorced at least once. "There no longer seems to be much of a stigma attached to divorce; it is now seen as an unavoidable rite of passage," the researcher indicated. "Interviews with young adults suggest that they want their initial marriage to last, but are not particularly optimistic about that possibility. There is also evidence that many young people are moving toward embracing the idea of serial marriage, in which a person gets married two or three times, seeking a different partner for each phase of their adult life."[4] It is time that we begin to intensely focus on family values and reverse the trends that are being reported. It is our desire to see men and women taking personal responsibility in the commitments they have made toward one another and fighting to stay together rather than fighting with each other after they

---

3 "The State of Our Unions" Rutgers National Marriage Project, 1999
   "Smart Marriages, Happy Families Conference" of the Coalition for Marriage, Family and Couples Education in Arlington, Virginia.
4 Marriage and Divorce Statistics – The Barna Group. March 31, 2008, Blisstree.com

have separated. If you feel you are on a dead-end road and the only option you see is divorce, consider your options and talk to someone you can trust before you make any decisions that you may regret for years to come.

In our current political climate, there are a number of state legislatures that have recently or are currently debating the recognition of marriage as an institution. In this climate many voter ballots define marriage as being between one man and one woman, while at the same time companies offer benefits to unmarried partners that are identical to the benefits employers provide married couples. According to ballotpedia.org, twenty-nine states have passed state constitutional amendments banning gay marriage, and there have been fifteen states with marriage-related ballot measures since 2006.[5] Marriage has been "on trial" in many states in recent years and it appears as if the institution of marriage will continue to be a politically divisive topic in the future.

We encourage you to make a *lifelong commitment* with your spouse to avoid becoming another statistical entry in a divorce report. If you are in your first marriage, make it your only marriage. If you are in a subsequent marriage, turn your previous failures into success and break the cycle; make this your last marriage. Do it for yourself, do it for your spouse, and just as important, do it for your kids.

Turn Poor Examples and Experiences Into a Positive Outcome

We have all made some pretty dumb choices, haven't we? I have no problem admitting it! You may have purchased a product that you saw on television or in a store ad that claims to melt pounds away with no effort, or perhaps you've invested in a get-rich-quick scheme that seems too good to be true.

If you haven't figured it out yet, if it sounds too good to be true, most likely it is a scam. However, we have all at some point in time purchased one of those Ab Whatevers that flattens your belly with absolutely no effort or dieting, or we've sent money in for a how-to CD, only to realize later that we have been ripped off. In almost every situation, when we look back on it, we ask ourselves how we could have fallen for that. You may ask yourself, "Why didn't I realize it was a scam?" or "How could I

---

5 http://ballotpedia.org/wiki/index.php/Marriage_ballot_measures

have been so naïve?" We lost three thousand, five hundred dollars in a refinance deal that looked so promising and was endorsed by people we personally knew and respected, but the deal turned out to be a scam and we have never recovered our money. In retrospect, the signs were clear but we didn't recognize them for what they were.

The positive outcome of becoming victimized by scams is a heightened awareness. The next time you walk through a sporting goods store and see the latest and greatest product claiming to melt away the pounds with little or no effort, you buy a good set of running shoes and a treadmill instead. Instead of signing up for the get-rich-quick seminar at the local convention center, you invest your time and money in something more stable and reliable. You address your debt load and develop a responsible budget that you can live with and that addresses and reduces your debt. When you do these things, you recall your bad experiences and apply the lessons learned to avoid repeating the mistakes.

If you've ever tried to lick a frozen metal fence or a lamppost when you were a kid, chances are you cringe inwardly when it snows outside or you see icicles forming on the chain link fence in the backyard. You learned from your previous mistake and even the slightest reminder of that situation causes you to pause and think before you proceed.

This is exactly what we need to do to break the cycle of divorce. If you have been previously divorced, you need to be reminded of the reasons that caused your relationship to splinter and avoid repeating those mistakes or choices. You also need to have checks and balances in your life that help you to stay accountable and avoid compromising situations.

If you are in your first (and we hope only) marriage, think about some people you know who have been divorced. Do you know what led to the break-up of the marriage? Perhaps it was infidelity. You can evaluate your own life and make sure you keep yourself accountable to your spouse. Perhaps it was an addiction to pornography. Again, evaluate your own life and consider getting a filter on your Internet to help you avoid the temptation of pornography. Perhaps what led to their divorce was an alcohol or drug addiction. Evaluate your own personal behaviors and habits; if you find yourself drinking in excess, challenge yourself to give up alcohol for a period of time. What you want to do is identify the behavior that led to the divorce and learn from the past mistakes, and take the necessary steps to avoid repeating those same behaviors.

If we don't learn from the mistakes that others make, often the only other option available is to make those same mistakes ourselves and suffer the consequences. One thing a mentor of mine told me once is to learn as many lessons from the mistakes of others that I possibly can. The price is always higher when one pays it himself.

> When you choose to stay married, you build a legacy for your children to cherish.

When I wanted to begin driving, my mother and I were discussing the issue of buying a car. When she made it crystal clear that she was not going to buy me a car and I wasn't responsible enough to drive yet, I asked instead for a new bicycle. I told her that if she would buy the bike for me, I would feel so indebted to her that I would take better care of it. I would value it more.

She told me in return that if she bought me the bike, I wouldn't appreciate it as much as I would if I bought it myself, and I would neglect it. However, if I bought it with my own money, I would better understand the value of it and would then take better care of it. You can probably imagine whose opinion won out in the end.

I bought the bike and I realized that she was right. I did value it more. You see, the price is always higher, or seems higher, when you pay the price yourself. Thanks Mom, for another valuable life lesson!

There is a Better Way

If you are a child of divorce, that's all you need to be . . . a *child* of divorce. What happened to your parents' relationship is not your fault. It is not your responsibility and it's not your burden to bear. You can be determined to provide a better family relationship and more stability for your kids, and you can ensure that they avoid some of the pain you had to suffer.

When you choose to stay married, you build a legacy for your children to cherish. You set the example for your children to follow and you teach them that it is possible to overcome challenges and obstacles in their lives. You demonstrate tenacity and persistence, which are valuable traits for them to develop in life. As you both work together to solve the myriad of problems you face, you send a strong message to your children and you improve their emotional stability. With each problem or challenge you conquer, you strengthen your marriage and attain a deeper level of commitment and happiness.

When you choose to stay married, you experience the joy and benefits that are a part of family tradition. Whether it is holiday traditions or simple traditions you share on a daily basis, the stability you can have in your life when you stay married is something that many people desire but never achieve. These traditions can be carried on by your children long into the future.

Another benefit of staying married is that as you share the many challenges of life with your life-long partner, you change and grow together. Neither of you are the same person you were on the day you married, and as you maintain a loving relationship, you develop and deepen your relationship together, resulting in more self-confidence and assurance.

With all of these benefits, there are also the financial benefits of remaining married. You most likely have assets that you have worked for and have accumulated together, that are in both of your names. These assets may include a house(s), cars, stocks and bonds, retirement accounts, or other investment assets. A divorce most likely will necessitate the liquidation of these assets and may result in a division of all the assets that you both jointly own. Add to this the financial impact of maintaining separate living residences, the duplication of vehicles or other life necessities, and perhaps even child support. We would never suggest that you remain together simply for financial reasons, but there are certainly financial benefits to remaining married.

We implore you to make the commitment to one another and make your marriage work. This isn't to say that you won't have problems and your kids won't be affected by some of the choices you make, but commit to yourself and to your family that your kids will always be able to come home to both Mom and Dad. Commit to doing everything in your power to cultivate an amazing marriage. It's worth the effort!

Debby and I must now make a special note regarding our parents. We love our parents dearly, and nothing they have done or would do can change that. We don't think any less of them because of the choices they have made in the past and we don't want our readers to judge them based on their decisions and choices. However, we don't want our kids to grow up wondering, like I did, what it would be like to live in a home with both Mom and Dad around.

If you've been divorced, strive to keep relationships between you and your previous spouse open and friendly. If there are kids involved, it is crucial that you keep things civil. If you loved each other enough at one time to get married and have kids, certainly you can care enough for one another to stay friendly for the sake of the children. While it is understandable that there is a high cost you pay when you get divorced, both monetarily and emotionally, the price the children pay in terms of broken relationships and missed opportunities far outweighs what the husband or wife pay.

Debby and I are both determined to break the cycle of divorce in our families. You too, can choose to break the cycle, stay the course, and stay married. It's up to you . . . you can do it!

Biblical Perspective

It takes work to produce an amazing marriage. I don't think anyone would debate that—hard work and an uncommon commitment toward one another. The Bible tells us to "take up our cross daily." Now, Jesus isn't referring to marriage here, and I certainly don't want to draw a picture of your spouse as being a burden; but, in a similar manner, we are to shoulder our responsibilities to make our marriage work on a daily basis. God has ordained marriage and intends for us to remain with our spouse forever. Mark 10:6-9 says, "But at the beginning of creation God made them male and female. For this reason a man will leave his father and mother and be united to his wife, and the two will become one flesh. So they are no longer two, but one. Therefore what God has joined together, let man not separate."

All sin is equal in God's economy, but as our knowledge of right and wrong increases, so does our accountability. Hebrews 5:11-14 is a call to spiritual growth and verse 14 talks about how we as Christians increase our ability to distinguish right from wrong. In the context of marriage, as we increase our knowledge and understanding of what He says regarding relationships, I believe we are held to a higher level of accountability. Similarly, as we grow in our relationship with Him and we mature in our faith (2 Peter 3:18), the Holy Spirit reveals to us areas of sin that as a new Christian, we may not have recognized as being sin. Furthermore, as James states it, "to him that knoweth to do good and doeth it not, to him it is sin." (KJV)

Our goal when we started this project was to encourage you and to share our experiences, so perhaps you could apply the hard lessons we have learned through our mistakes and avoid making some of those same mistakes in your marriage. Perhaps we could save you the pain of experiencing some of the trials we have gone through, as you apply some of the principles we present.

In John 15:4 Jesus says, "Abide in me and I in you." (KJV) You've probably heard many preachers talk about this passage and what Christ meant when He said "abide in Me." To abide means to be still or to stay. It means to meditate on Him and allow His word to penetrate your heart.

Sometimes life can be so hectic and the pressures we put on ourselves to fulfill the expectations of others can overwhelm us. We have responsibilities at work, at church, with a small group, our kids' school, a volunteer organization, and many other areas that we often find ourselves giving our spouse and our family the leftovers of our time.

If you heed the words of Christ and abide in Him first, and then expand that to abide in and focus on your spouse, what a difference you could see in your marriage. Imagine for a moment how meaningful a few moments every day alone with your spouse would be. What would that do for your relationship? Imagine what that would mean in terms of building your bond of love and your commitment to one another. What would it do for your kids to see Mom and Dad truly respecting and loving each other, in a world where they see the exact opposite on television and in the movies? Learn to be still and enjoy alone time with your spouse. It will enhance your relationship on many levels.

When I think of abiding in Christ, I think of Mary sitting at the feet of Jesus soaking up His every word, completely unaware of the activities going on around her. Spiritually, we need to do that. We need to sit at His feet and soak up His every word. We need to abide in Him and in His word, and be open to His leading and direction for our life. When we are in the center of His will, we find that our other relationships are more meaningful. When we are in the center of His will, He can reveal to us His plans and direction for our life.

For our spouse, we should do the same. We need to "sit at their feet and soak up their every word" and focus our time and attention on them. When our purpose is to serve our spouse and meet their every need, willingly, we demonstrate our love and unbridled commitment to one another.

Jesus demonstrated His humility when He washed the feet of His disciples. Peter initially had the attitude that there was no way Jesus would wash his feet. John 13 records these events and in verse 7 Peter told Jesus that He would never wash Peter's feet. He (Peter) was too proud to allow Christ to wash his feet because he didn't understand what Jesus meant in this act of humility. When Jesus told Peter that if he didn't allow Him to wash his feet then Peter could have no part of Christ, Peter proclaimed, "Then wash my hands and head as well, Lord, not just my feet!" (John 13:9) In the end, Jesus washed the feet of all His disciples and modeled the love and humility we are to have toward one another.

If you have never washed the feet of your spouse, let us encourage you to do so. What an act of love! What an act of humility, that you would demonstrate your love for your spouse in this manner. Set aside an evening where you two are alone together and follow the example Jesus set for us. Wash one another's feet. You'll be glad you did.

Chapter 6

Unmet Expectations

"To you I give everything because you expect nothing."
~ Dr. Joseph Sims

Unmet expectations and the inability to clearly communicate your feelings may have the potential to destroy your marriage. At the very least, unmet expectations can lead to hurt, resentment, and arguments that could easily be avoided if expectations were clearly identified in advance. When we have expectations of someone that continually go unmet, it is next to impossible to maintain a positive, growing, and nurturing relationship with that person.

Over the years, when people have asked us what we thought were the biggest roadblocks to a successful marriage, our answer has been consistent: unmet expectations and poor communication. You can boil down most of the challenges you face in your marriage, at work, and in your other relationships and see that they most likely fall into one of these two categories. Unmet expectations were a major stumbling block in our own marriage as we started out. Even now, we often find ourselves evaluating how well we communicate our expectations to one another. It's a continuous effort to place a high priority on clarifying expectations.

One problem with unmet expectations is that we may not even know what our own expectations of others are. It may be that we have never identified what it is we expect of others, specifically our spouse, so it is difficult to communicate those expectations to others. If expectations are not communicated, they cannot be met.

It will be a personal journey for each person to decide and figure out what they expect out of their marriage and what they expect from their spouse. You may decide to set some time aside to think about your expectations and write them down. To begin to identify what it is you expect of yourself and of your spouse, set aside a period of time and reflect on expectations. Write things down as they come to mind, and organize your thoughts. This would be a great exercise to do on a weekend get-away, just the two of you. Once personal expectations have been iden-tified and clarified in your own mind, the two of you need to come to-gether and identify the common expectations. There should be a number of things that are important to both of you, and you should discuss these shared expectations and how they could be carried out in your marriage.

You should talk about the differences you may have and set goals for your marriage based on those expectations. It is so easy for expectations to be misunderstood and misinterpreted. Having a discussion about the specific expectations will allow you both to ask questions for clarifica-tion, questions that will help avoid disappointment in the future. As you explain your expectations to one another, be as specific as possible. A lack of detail can quickly set a course for disappointment.

Just as important as clearly explaining your viewpoint in terms that the other person can understand, you need to listen intently to what they are saying in return. Listening to what someone has to say and truly understanding their viewpoint is not always easily accomplished, but it is an important aspect of establishing expectations. Many times what a person says and what they mean are two different things and the result is usually unmet expectations and disappointment. At some point in the conversation it is wise to repeat back to one another what you under-stand to have been said and agreed upon. This simple step of repeating back what you have heard and understood may identify areas that need to be further clarified.

Whether you realize it or not, you bring expectations into your mar-riage that you may not have been able to identify prior to getting married. We recently had dinner with an older couple celebrating fifty-two years of marriage, and I am now reminded of something he said. We were talk-ing about our oldest daughter who has known her boyfriend since they were seven years old, and Debby commented that they really know each other. This gentleman, Garland, said "No they don't. You don't really know someone until you start living with them." That is so true. We think we know one another, but it isn't until you share a roof and a bed with someone that you truly begin to get to know who they really are. It is also at that point when you realize you have expectations of your spouse that perhaps you didn't understand prior to getting married or living together.

When you get married, you bring certain expectations into the re-lationship from your childhood that perhaps you didn't realize existed.

More than likely you picked up some things from watching your parents and the way they interacted with one another, and you bring some of these expectations of how you believe your marriage should be to the altar. These expectations are based on what you experienced growing up, and can be from both a positive and a negative influence. There are many ways that one can come to have these expectations. Influence comes from parents, siblings, friends, co-workers, the media, and numerous other sources.

You both bring these expectations or preconceived ideas of what marriage should look like into your relationship. Some of these expectations may be revealed in premarital counseling, but there are bound to be some expectations that aren't discussed or discovered until after you return from your honeymoon and you settle into your routines.

As we have discussed earlier in the chapter on communication, we used to have a full-blown, drag-down fight about every three months during the first four or five years of our marriage. As unmet expectations built up over a period of time our pent-up anger also built up until we couldn't contain it any longer. One or both of us would unleash a barrage of attacks at the other that lasted well into the night. As we sat looking at each other through sheer exhaustion, usually around 2:00 AM, we would begin to make promises that sounded good at the time but were never achieved over the next couple of months, thus beginning the cycle of unmet expectations yet again. We never seemed to be lacking for things to fight about!

This went on until we realized we had no idea how to communicate with each other and we began counseling. In our counseling sessions we learned how to express our feelings so that we didn't attack one another. We learned how to clearly explain what our expectations were and learned how to listen to one another. As we slowly began to talk about the hurt we both felt for years, we both realized that we had much larger expectations of each other than we ever communicated clearly.

There are two main points that I clearly recall from our counseling sessions that we incorporate on a consistent basis. One thing our counselor stressed over and over again is the need for me to listen to Debby when she speaks. To allow her time to clearly express herself, in any manner she feels she needs to, and for me to listen without interrupting. That is the key—I cannot interrupt, I can't explain, I can't be defensive, and I can't argue. It is her time to talk and say whatever she feels she needs to say, without me cutting her off and arguing or defending my position. Now, I do have my opportunity to talk as well, and I can explain or clarify why or when something happened, but it isn't a debate session. Of course, this works both ways. There are times when I need to talk and it is her turn to listen.

One of the most important components of clarifying expectations is open and specific communication. We have learned how to communicate with one another in a way that allows the other to understand what it is we are saying. This helps us to avoid falling prey to unmet expectations and the resulting disappointment, though we do miss the mark at times. When we fail to communicate as we know we should and it results in disappointment, we typically recognize this before things get out of hand. The key is that we have learned to recognize our mistakes earlier than we have in the past, and we know enough to take the necessary steps to clarify and rectify the problems.

The second point that our counselor made very clear is that sometimes I need to hold Debby. Take her in my arms and just hold her. Words don't need to be used, and in some cases, it is best not to say anything. Debby will sometimes push me away and tell me that she doesn't want me to hold her, but I know those are the times when I need to hold her the most. These are the times when she needs reassurance that everything will be okay and that I love her and am here for her regardless of the circumstance or the fight that we are in.

Anger was our natural response to unmet expectations. The best thing we have learned to do to combat the anger and fighting is to find out what the expectations of our spouse are well in advance so we have plenty of opportunity to meet or exceed the expectations. If we need clarification, there is time to get the clarification to avoid disappointment.

Debby and I talk all the time. Not necessarily three hour conversations, but constant communication. Ten minutes here, twenty minutes there, and we typically find that we are discussing something to do with our kids; who is picking Abby up from the gym, who is running the school carpool, who's going to the grocery store, etc.

Our days are usually planned in advance for logistical purposes and if anything changes, we just make a quick call or send a text message to clarify things. We have realized an increased need for better communication now that Debby has started working part-time. We know that with our busy lives, we need to manage our time and communication so as to ensure harmony in the house.

There are times when we think that we haven't connected or talked enough and it's time to take a date night or go out for a cup of coffee just to reconnect and establish expectations. We have four children; the oldest recently graduated from high school, our second oldest is a senior in high school, and the younger two are in middle school. They seem to take us in completely different directions on a daily basis. With their various activities, our jobs, and other ministries and volunteer organizations we are involved with, we need to clearly communicate expectations. When this doesn't happen as it should, the result can be short responses and quick-to-anger attitudes cropping up. It's easy for us to recognize the lack of clear communication and to see our attitudes turning sour and we take some much needed alone time to reconnect.

Our kids have learned the value of clear expectations as well. As we were writing this portion of the book, we took a weekend retreat to Leavenworth, Washington. We were due home sometime Sunday afternoon but we were not sure what time we would arrive and told our kids it would be sometime in the afternoon. As we were on the way home, our oldest daughter called and wanted to know if we were on the way yet and what time we thought we would get home. She said she knew we expected the house to be clean when we got home, and she wanted to know how much time they had to clean it. The kids knew our expectations; they just wanted clarification of the timeframe. Our desire is that our kids learn the value of clarifying expectations and learn to take these lessons with them when they go to college and when they marry. We'd much rather they learn this through our journey and apply it in their lives as opposed to going through the years of anger and frustration that we endured.

We recently had a disagreement about something regarding our children. The issue at hand was an outing we allowed one of our teenage daughters to go on and who would be picking her up afterward. As we were discussing this, after neither of us had picked her up on time, we both came to the conclusion that we had failed to properly clarify our expectations up front, and if we had done so, we could have avoided the disappointment we both felt.

The first step in avoiding unmet expectations is to establish what our expectations are in advance. We need to identify what our expectations are and then communicate them clearly. Talking through our expectations with one another and agreeing in advance what the end result should look like is extremely important.

It is so easy for expectations to be misunderstood and even misinterpreted. Having a discussion to identify what we expect of each other in different situations can help us avoid conflict and disappointment. As we explain our expectations, we need to be as specific as possible. A lack of detail can quickly set a course toward disappointment.

In addition to these shared expectations, you can also talk about the differences in your personal expectations. There are bound to be things that are more or less important to one of you based on your upbringing, family traditions, or any number of other outside influences. There may be family traditions that you have experienced while growing up that you want to make sure to carry out in your own marriage. Likewise, there are bound to be family traditions or practices that you want to make sure you do not carry on in your own family, and you hope that these traditions die a quick and tragic death somewhere.

As you share and discuss these expectations, create goals for your marriage that are based on those individual expectations. It is important to find the common ground you share, as well as identify and discuss any expectations that you identified that the other did not have on his or her list. You may identify an item or goal on this individual list that may have caused disappointment in the past that has not been thoroughly understood by your spouse. By identifying these expectations, you may very well be preventing future disagreements and disappointments.

This identification and discussion of goals and expectations is something that every married couple can do, regardless of how long they have been married. It would obviously be beneficial if you had this type of goal-setting before getting married, but if you are already married and have been together for many years and have not yet really clarified your shared goals and expectations, this is something that we encourage you to do as soon as possible. Once you identify your goals and expectations and you talk about how you can implement these expectations, write out a plan to reach your goals. If you have been living your married life together without clearly identified expectations and goals, you should see immediate changes and benefits with this exercise.

Each time our expectations go unmet, it can result in hurt feelings, disappointment, bitterness, and anger. We may have these feelings slowly build up within us, and oftentimes we don't recognize it until it is too late. When a dam on a river breaks, it is usually not the result of a specific event, but erosion or weakening of the structure over time. Oftentimes a hairline fracture can occur and not be noticed by a safety inspection. Over time, that small fracture grows bigger and bigger as the water pressure builds, and eventually the concrete begins to separate along the fracture line. This sets off a chain reaction throughout the structure and could lead to a complete failure of the dam.

Resentment is often a slow process that begins with unmet expectations. Like a dam that weakens under pressure, our relationship weakens over time as we face continued disappointment. One may even find themselves coming to expect disappointment because of the track record of their spouse. If you are continually facing disappointment, you may find yourself lowering your expectations rather than clarifying them to your spouse. Chances are great that if you would simply clarify what you want or need, these needs would be met and you wouldn't need to lower your expectations.

Lowered expectations usually result in lower outcomes. If your spouse continues to miss the bar in terms of your expectations and you continually lower the bar to compensate, you may find yourself in a downward spiral of increasing disappointment and resentment.

> Resentment is often a slow process that begins with unmet expectations.

When we got married, Debby had an ideal concept of what she thought a family was supposed to be like. Growing up, her dad was always home by 4:30 PM, so she had this expectation when we got married I would be home consistently like this. However, I was working my way up the career ladder in a retail business and eventually I had to work varied shifts. Sometimes I would need to stay at work longer than I was scheduled, and I would need to call and let Debby know I would be late. In my mind, I was doing what I needed to do to provide for my family, even if it meant putting in extra time to be noticed by my superiors for future promotions. In her mind, I was putting work first and depriving her and the family of my time.

After several years of disappointment and unmet expectations, she finally figured out how to communicate to me that all I needed to do was to call her well in advance and let her know I would be late, or that there had been a change to my schedule. Rather than waiting to call until the time I was expected to be home, as I so often did, she explained that if I would only call her in advance and let her know that I would be late it would alleviate some of her anger and frustration. Yes, she still got upset at times when I would be consistently late coming home from work, but knowing in advance that there was a possibility of this happening, she was able to rearrange her activities and the expectations she had of me. I finally figured out that it was important that I avoid last-minute changes and that I clearly communicate with her. Sounds pretty simple now, but we dealt with disappointment time and time again.

I expected her to understand that I was doing what I needed to do to provide for my family and she expected me to understand that I needed to be home. For a period of about one year I was working for a manager who seemed intent on giving me the worst possible shifts and it was extremely difficult on both Debby and me. It got to the point that I hated having to call her to say I would be late because she always got angry. So, rather than risk a fight on the phone, I began not calling and just showing up late, trying to blame it on bad traffic. Let me tell you, the traffic excuse is only good for so long, and when we were living in a rental house less than two miles from my work place, well, it was nonexistent.

If only we knew then what we know now, we would have had many more peaceful nights of sleep! If we had taken the time to explain to each other our perspective, we would have reached a middle ground of understanding. I would have better understood how important it was for her that I get home at a particular time, and she would have better understood my need to do whatever I felt it took to be successful at work. The majority of the time that I had to work a longer shift was truly out of my control and not a matter of choices I made.

One thing I learned to do to help me manage my time better was to plan on leaving thirty minutes before my shift ended. If I was scheduled to work until 6:00, I arranged my work load for a 5:30 completion time and let my employees know that I was off at 5:30. It seemed that on many occasions my employees would bring up a question or a problem at the end of the day, expecting an immediate solution, and it was typically as I was gathering my things to leave for the day. By making this small time adjustment, I was able to complete my work and still allow time for those last minute requests. When I did this, I was usually able to leave at 6:00 as I was scheduled to do, without having to extend my work day to handle problems that cropped up at the end of the day.

I can honestly say that at no time did I ever use work as an escape outlet because I didn't want to be home, though I know a number of people who have done that. For some, working longer hours is a better alternative than going home to face a spouse and deal with a bad relationship. We hope that this doesn't describe you.

When expectations continue to go unmet, resentment and anger builds up. Anger is often the result of unmet or unfulfilled expectations and grows each time expectations are not met. Sometimes we may direct our anger at a person who is completely innocent, but happens to be in our path at the time. It may be that your spouse has unmet expectations from work or another friend and you are the unfortunate recipient of that anger.

Oftentimes in a relationship we misunderstand the residual effect of someone's anger. We may fail to realize that they are angry at someone or something else and we assume that their anger is directed toward us. In some cases, this may cause us to become defensive or even hostile ourselves, perpetuating the problem or creating a problem that never even existed between us. If we don't communicate our feelings or disappointments, we can misdirect our anger to innocent bystanders, which could lead to additional conflict and resentment. Communication is important in discovering where the anger is rooted and what action needs to take place to settle the conflict and eliminate resentment.

We would be remiss in discussing unmet expectations if we didn't include a section on envy. Recently Debby shared this example with me. A woman had lunch with one of her girlfriends who had recently received a beautiful diamond necklace as a gift from her husband. It was one of those special "just because" gifts that wasn't tied to any specific occasion. This woman had commented that her husband hadn't bought her a "just because" gift in a very long time and this began to bother her. She was envious of her girlfriend and the necklace she had been given.

In a very short amount of time she began to expect something from her husband and actually became quite bitter as more time went on. At no time did she share her frustrations with her husband or the fact that she felt neglected in not receiving spontaneous gifts. Eventually this erupted into a serious fight between her and her husband, and he had no idea what was causing her to be so angry. When she was able to communicate how she felt, he realized that he needed to demonstrate his love for her through notes of appreciation and gifts of love. She knew that he would not be able to afford to buy her a diamond like the one her friend received, but the fact that she wasn't getting anything at all was what led to her bitterness. Looking back, she feels embarrassed that she responded the way she did. However, it was important that the two of them communicated on the issue and through this experience he has discovered that what she needs and craves is his attention and little reminders of his love.

In virtually every area of our lives, there are expectations that our spouse or other people have of us. It is crucial that we identify what those expectations are and that we clearly communicate to others what we expect of them. Our relationships will be far more productive and fulfilling when expectations are clarified.

In my company there are several different evaluations that we use to critique our employees. As a supervisor, I have always felt that it is very important to provide a blank evaluation form to every employee when he or she is newly promoted to a higher level of responsibility. I clearly explain the criterion upon which they will be evaluated, which allows them to focus on doing the right things and eliminates surprises when they are evaluated. Personally, I prefer knowing in advance what my business leaders expect of me so I can fulfill and exceed those expectations, and I do the same for my employees. It is important that they have a clear understanding of expectations, which actually improves the evaluation process.

We obviously don't write an evaluation on our spouse, but the same principle can be applied in marriage. The more we clarify expectations on the front end, the better we can meet and exceed those expectations, and enjoy the benefits of an amazing marriage.

Biblical Perspective

It takes work to produce an amazing marriage. That may be the understatement of the book. Whether the expectations we have of one another that go unmet are major ordeals or simply minor annoyances, God can give us the understanding and forgiveness that is required. We read in 2 Corinthians 9:8, "God is able to make all grace abound to you, so that in all things at all times, having all that you need, you will abound in every good work." (NIV) We all endure the pain of unmet expectations at some point and it is encouraging to know that God's grace is sufficient for our every need.

Sometimes our expectations are materialistic in nature, and yet Paul encourages believers to value things of God more than things of the earth. "Godliness with contentment is great gain. For we brought nothing into the world, and we can take nothing out of it." (1 Tim. 6:6–7 NIV) Paul also said "I have learned to be content whatever the circumstances. I know what it is to be in need, and I know what it is to have plenty." (Phil 4:11–12) If we could emulate this attitude, some of our materialistic expectations may not be as important as they once were.

Too often, when a couple discusses unmet expectations, harsh words and a biting tongue have the potential to do more damage to the relationship than the initial disappointment. James chapter 3 tells us that the tongue is a small thing but can do great damage. Those who control their tongue control themselves in every other way. The tongue is full of wickedness and can destroy. If you can learn to hold your tongue, listen more and say less, you may find that resolution to your unmet expectations comes sooner than you expect.

We addressed unmet expectations from a standpoint of wanting more or wanting what others may have. Hebrews 13:5 discusses contentment this way: "Keep your lives free from the love of money and be content with what you have, because God has said never will I leave you; never will I forsake you." (NIV)

If you or your spouse suffers the pain of unmet expectations day after day and there appears to be no end in sight, you may begin to lose interest in making your marriage work and you may think you are in a dead-end marriage. You may believe that divorce is the best, if not the only, option for you; and you may find yourself withdrawing from your spouse and building a wall around your emotions. Don't allow your disappointments to grow into depression and self-pity, and don't allow yourself to withdraw emotionally.

> 'For I know the plans I have for you,' declares the Lord, 'plans to prosper you and not to harm you, plans to give you hope and a future.'

Proverbs 13:12 does say that, "Hope deferred makes the heart sick, but a dream fulfilled is a tree of life." It is important that you address your concerns with your spouse in as clear a manner as possible, without blaming him or her for the circumstances you find yourself in. It may be that your spouse is not aware of your feelings and you owe it to them to make your feelings known. If you don't make known your feelings, you may continue to face anger and frustration on a daily basis, which could lead to bitterness and even culminate in resentment.

Don't fall for the trap of contentment if you are in a relationship where you have lost all hope. If this describes you, renew your hope in the Lord and ask Him to give you the courage to stay in the fight and fight to make your marriage amazing. I can't help but refer once again to Jeremiah 29: 11–13, "'For I know the plans I have for you,' declares the Lord, 'plans to prosper you and not to harm you, plans to give you hope and a future. Then you will call upon Me and come and pray to Me, and I will listen to you. You will seek Me and find Me when you seek Me with all your heart.'" (NIV) He has a plan for your life and part of that plan is to give you both hope and a future.

Unmet expectations can occur on a consistent and regular basis in your marriage, or it could be due to an occasional oversight on the part of you or your spouse. Wherever you fall on the spectrum, practice clear and concise communication with one another and commit to meeting the needs of each other to the very best of your ability.

Chapter 7

Living Beyond Mediocrity

"I've missed more than 9,000 shots in my career. I've lost almost 300 games; 26 times I've been trusted to take the game winning shot and missed. I've failed over and over and over again in my life. And that is why I succeed."

~ Michael Jordan

Mediocre: Of only ordinary or moderate quality; neither good nor bad; barely adequate, rather poor or inferior; second-rate; average; fair. Characterless, common, dull, indifferent, inferior, tolerable, insignificant, ordinary.[1]

The above definitions paint quite a dismal picture. I can't think of anything in my life that I would want described by any of these labels. I think the most impactful definition of mediocre is an "attitude of indifference." Sadly, marriages the world over, can fall into one or more of the above definitions, which was part of our motivation to write our book. As we interact with some of our friends and some of the parents of our children's friends, we all too often talk with people who are locked in marriages that can be described by some of the above definitions.

As it relates to your marriage, don't settle for mediocrity. Don't fall for the misconception that marriage is not worth the investment or that it is not worth the time and effort that an amazing marriage requires. We have spent the past several years talking with couples and helping them discover the potential of an amazing marriage in their own relationship. As we talk to married and divorced couples, we find that one of the biggest threats to marriage is mediocrity and the lack of hope.

Have you ever received an evaluation at work that rated you as "satisfactory" or, worse yet, "average?" What exactly is average anyway, and who wants to be average? No one that I know. Does average mean that exactly half the employees are better than you and half the employees are worse than you? And what if you make just one more mistake today than everyone else? What if you missed a deadline or were rejected on

---

1 http://dictionary.reference.com/browse/mediocre

a sales call? Would that drive your evaluation down to the dreaded "below average" mark?

Are you constantly living in fear that if your boss disapproves of your work, then you will be associated with the lower half of the employees in your company or work force? If this is you, you may discover that this can put so much pressure on you that you may actually lose productivity because you are fearful of making mistakes.

Nobody should live with that kind of pressure. Nobody should approach work every day fearful that they need to perform in a certain way to avoid falling below the halfway mark. Nobody needs to live in fear that their boss will scrutinize their work, find all their faults, and continually wonder if their evaluation hangs in the balance. It would be hard to find the motivation to continue.

Wouldn't it be easier to just throw in the towel and quit trying? Perhaps you would lose what motivation you had to begin with and, as your performance slips, you would begin to just not care any longer. If that were to happen, then there would be no pressure to perform. There would be no desire to improve. You would simply show up for work day after day, doing the exact same thing with the exact same effort, and you would get the exact same result.

If you continued down this path for any extended amount of time, you would find that you just don't care anymore about what your boss or co-workers say, and you may actually become accepting of the label "average." You may not openly embrace it and recognize it, but your lack of action in making changes to break the cycle basically equates to acceptance. It becomes a "no-brainer" job with little or no expectations. You go to work day after day and under-achieve, yet you don't recognize it for what it is. Your performance-based salary increases are a thing of the past, yet that doesn't even motivate you to change.

Now, I don't think anyone wakes up and tells themselves that they are going to go to work today to be a poor performer, but this is the situation many people find themselves in over time and they either don't care or don't know how to break the cycle.

Here's the real question: Who would settle for that kind of performance? Who can be motivated day after day to go to a job and perform in such a manner? Who wants to always be living in the shadow of the high-achievers? I have to ask myself, who wants to be labeled as average and what kind of person would be okay with that?

Unfortunately, many people approach not only their job in this manner, but their marriage as well. They may have started out with the enthusiasm and passion of newlyweds and may have poured themselves into making their marriage the very best that it could be, but then something happened. Something changed as time marched on. Perhaps it was a specific incident that one could look back on and identify, but more often than not, it is a slow erosion—a gradual drifting apart that's hardly even noticeable until it's too late.

For many couples, they have unique and separate interests that occupy large amounts of their time. Whether it's a sport, craft, hobby, or even your children, it is so easy to find yourselves spending an increasing amount of time away from each other. While it is important for couples to maintain their unique identities and interests, and it's important for each partner to be able to have time to enjoy them, it can have damaging consequences if you don't manage your time properly and keep things in balance and in perspective.

> The path that leads to an amazing marriage is a long and often winding road but it can be a very exciting and fulfilling journey.

I am positive there is not a soul on this planet who would say that they hope for their marriage to be mediocre—a marriage of low quality, inferiority, or of no value. No one aspires to have this kind of marriage and yet as we look around us, there are many marriages that are just that: mediocre. Not necessarily bad, but not really good either. Just average.

Time has a way of lulling to sleep the passion you once had for your spouse and replacing it with complacency and apathy, if you let it. The mindset that this is as good as it gets can creep in and you might decide to acknowledge that, call it quits, and go in search of something more. If you fall in that trap, you are lowering the bar of excellence in your marriage and a marriage death sentence has been handed down. Is this the path you would choose for your marriage? Of course not.

One thing is for sure, an amazing marriage is definitely worth the effort and the work that it takes. The path that leads to an amazing marriage is a long and often winding road but it can be a very exciting and fulfilling journey. As you begin to discover the expectations of your spouse and begin meeting their needs the way they expect them to be met, your marriage will be well on the way toward excellence. The law of reciprocity will be set in motion, and as you meet the needs of your spouse, you will begin to realize your needs being met in return.

Mediocrity is the easy way out. It takes no effort to be mediocre. Anybody can do it and do it well. But why be like everyone else? Why be the norm? Why not prove the statistics wrong? Stay in your marriage, love your spouse the way they need you to love them, and achieve what we believe is possible for you—the amazing marriage we all desire.

We have talked to many couples who have drifted apart over the years of their marriage and have less in common now than when they got married, and who spend far less time together now than they ever have before. In most of these marriages, there are problems that result from this time apart. It is usually not evident at first, but over time their interests go in separate directions and they drift apart.

If you find yourself in a relationship similar to this, make a conscious decision to reverse the path your marriage is currently on. Identify things that you can do on a daily basis that will have an impact on your spouse and that may turn your marriage around in a whole new direction. Make a point to identify activities you can do together to spend time with one another. Schedule some time on a consistent basis where you can both set aside your individual interests and hobbies and come together for some shared experiences. You may find this awkward in the beginning and you may think there just aren't many things you both enjoy, but as you put your mind to it you will discover mutual interests.

There are a number of things you can do with little or no money, so don't let your budget get in the way. Perhaps taking a walk through your neighborhood, along the water's edge, or in your local mall would be a good place to start. Sharing a hot fudge sundae together at the local ice cream shop is an inexpensive routine you can begin that will give you the jumpstart you need. If the ice cream shop is in the mall, you can even walk off the extra calories together!

The point is simple, don't allow your relationship to become stale or filled with mediocrity. As we discussed in previous chapters, it is important to vary your routines and be spontaneous while setting aside time that the two of you share alone together on a regular basis. If you find yourself slowly drifting apart, adjust that rudder today and begin to slowly drift toward one another again.

Did you settle for mediocrity when you were dating? Of course you didn't. You wanted the very best woman or the very best man available.

You wanted your knight in shining armor to come and sweep you away, or perhaps your princess bride to steal your heart. You didn't just settle for the first guy that asked you out or the first girl that accepted your invitation to a movie.

If a date didn't work out so well and you sat at dinner with very little conversation, chances are you didn't ask for or accept a second date. So if you didn't settle for mediocrity then, why settle for mediocrity now? You have both made a lifelong commitment to one another, and you both deserve to enjoy the very best that your spouse has to offer.

Keep in mind the premise of chapter 1, Love is a *Choice*. If you choose to, you can choose to settle for a life and marriage of mediocrity. Or, if you choose, you can have the most amazing marriage you can imagine. More than likely, if you can imagine it, you can achieve it. You can choose to not only live above mediocrity, but you can choose to have the very best marriage possible. As we have said, the choices you make on a daily basis dictate the health and temperature of your marriage.

Building a marriage that can be labeled as amazing, or successful, will take hard work and perseverance. You can't achieve a marriage such as that by simply wanting it, or choosing it, but in order to achieve it you must make choices and sacrifices along the way. The primary reason that the overwhelming majority of people do not have marriages that can be described as abundant and fulfilling is the sheer amount of time and effort these marriages require. Unfortunately, it is easier to make choices that result in mediocrity rather than excellence.

Living a life of mediocrity means that you are short-changing yourself and your spouse! Make the choice to be the exception. Choose to be the couple in your realm of influence who everyone else wonders what it is that you have that they don't. Be the exception rather than the rule.

Trust us when we tell you that if you choose to have and live out an amazing marriage, you will stand out. People will recognize that something is different about you. People will ask you what you have that they don't have. You will need to be prepared to give an answer for what makes your marriage unique. Even the friends of your children will notice the unique closeness your family has and they will wonder what makes you different from their parents.

This past October, we took our son and a friend of his out trick-or-treating. While we were walking down the road, his friend suddenly said, "I love spending time with your family." Debby asked him why, and he said, "Well, your family has so much fun together and you all really love each other. That's cool." Pretty neat observation coming from an eleven-year-old! Unfortunately for him, his parents are divorced and he apparently sees a difference between his family life and ours.

It is important to remember that the quality of your marriage doesn't just affect the two of you; it affects your entire family. Your kids, if you have any, may not fully comprehend everything that goes on between the two of you, but they all understand and can recognize love. When you and your spouse truly love one another and continually put the other first, it makes a lasting impression on your children.

Are there times in your life when you have choices that are labeled "good," "better," and "best?" I was recently out shopping for a new lawn mower to replace the one that was stolen from our yard last summer. The lily, the lawnmower . . . I didn't realize until now how bad our neighborhood is becoming. As I went from store to store comparing the features and benefits, and then weighing them against the cost, I noticed that several different stores put these labels on many products. Rather than label something "Cheap, Easily Broken," they label it "Good." The next step up in quality may be more accurately labeled as "Affordable, Gets the Job Done" rather than "Better." The very best that they have to offer is appropriately labeled as "Best."

To be honest, I am quite the penny-pincher and have even been described by some as cheap. I prefer the label of frugal rather than cheap, but you get the picture. Depending on what I am shopping for, many times the "Affordable, Gets the Job Done" item is what I choose to buy. I don't always buy the very best product that is available, if a more affordable model meets our needs. On the same hand, though, I rarely ever buy the cheapest low-end model either.

However, when there is something that is truly important, or something I highly value, I can always justify purchasing the very best model that is available. For a lawn mower, a mattress, or a set of dishes, the very best that is available may not be necessary. When it comes to your marriage relationship, a relationship that should be truly important and highly regarded, you should only choose the very best model or option available. You have already selected your spouse, now choose the very best that you can when you have choices that impact the quality of your relationship.

Let's put it this way. If you were able to choose the spouse for your son or daughter to marry, what are some traits and characteristics you would choose? If you were able to hand-pick your son-in-law or daughter-in-law, wouldn't you only consider the very best that is available? Wouldn't you search high and low and pick out someone who would be the very best spouse, and who would be the very best parent for your grandchildren? You wouldn't even consider anything or anyone that was less than the best. You certainly wouldn't choose mediocrity. No parent would.

Once you have in your mind what characteristics and traits would be ideal for your child, compare those to what you yourself offer to your spouse in your own marriage. Are you living up to the traits and characteristics that you would choose for your child's spouse? Are you making choices in your life that are affecting your spouse and your family in a way that would be honoring and pleasing to you, if the roles were reversed? How easy it is for us to look at someone else and talk about what they should or should not do, without realizing that we are sometimes guilty of the very accusations we may be making toward others. When put in this light, we need to seriously examine ourselves and determine if we are living up to those high standards. After all, your spouse deserves your very best! Jessica Claire, a professional photographer says, "The best asset anyone has is the ability to be the best them."

Living out a marriage beyond mediocrity may not always be the easiest thing to do and the choices may be a bit more difficult, but the rewards are plentiful. Living beyond mediocrity may mean that you think of others before you think of yourself. It may mean giving or doing something for others before you take care of your own needs. It may mean that you have to sacrifice some of your time, talents, or treasures, to put the needs of your spouse before your own. It may mean that you strive for excellence rather than settle for good. Helen Keller once said, "The greatest danger for most of us is not that our aim is too high and we miss it, but that it is too low and we reach it."

When you live out your marriage beyond mediocrity, and you achieve the excellent marriage we are describing, you experience the complete joy and fulfillment that your marriage was designed to offer. Your relationship with your spouse is more meaningful and you truly desire to ensure his or her complete happiness. You will find yourself being primarily concerned with what you can do for your spouse and how you can fulfill their needs, and you will spend less time focused on your own needs. When you choose and commit to give everything you have to your marriage and you pursue a relationship of excellence, you are giving your spouse the most precious gift you can give—yourself.

It Takes Two

We understand that there are individuals reading this that recognize they want more out of their marriage, yet their husband or wife doesn't think or acknowledge that there is a problem. Perhaps your spouse is happy and content with your marriage the way it is, and is not interested in making any changes or improvements. You may have even suggested that you both seek marriage counseling, yet your spouse refuses to go. What then, you may be asking. How can you discover an amazing marriage if your spouse doesn't acknowledge any problems?

Just as it takes the two of you to make a truly amazing marriage, it will also take the two of you to revive your marriage and reverse the course of a mediocre marriage. If your marriage is currently failing, you cannot save it on your own. It will require a commitment from both partners to make this work, but you can certainly start the process even if your spouse doesn't recognize the need for improvements or if he or she refuses to participate. Don't allow his or her reluctance stand in the way of your decision to implement changes.

If your spouse refuses to go to a marriage counselor, talk to him or her and clearly express your concerns. Make sure that he or she fully understands, in specific detail, why you are unhappy or what you want to see changed in your relationship. This is the evaluation process we discussed in chapter 1. As you communicate your concerns with your spouse, be sure to do so in a respectful and loving manner, without laying the guilt or blame on your partner.

It very well may be that your spouse acknowledges that there are problems that need to be addressed, and may even acknowledge the fact that the two of you are not equipped to handle your problems alone, yet he or she is embarrassed and does not want to share any personal failures with anyone else. If this appears to be the case, gently explain that you would rather seek the advice and help from a professional counselor and you want to talk to someone outside of your circle of friends. Just mentioning this may remind him or her that the alternative solution may be that you seek advice from your friends, which may lead to unnecessary embarrassment once the details are shared.

Pride may be the obstacle that you need to remove before your spouse agrees to seek help from outside your marriage. Perhaps you can suggest that he or she see a counselor on their own first, to allow them to share some of their feelings and thoughts without you being present. They may find that it is easier to talk to someone they don't know, and who doesn't know your situation, and this could help them to discover how they can express their feelings and establish dialogue. Often times, there is a reluctance to talk about marital problems with someone while your spouse is present, and perhaps an introduction to counseling can be done on an individual basis. This will provide you both the opportunity to develop trust with your counselor, and then after time you can transition to counseling sessions together as a couple.

We highly encourage couples to have a mentor couple; a couple married for at least ten years and with a consistent and positive track record. This mentor couple would be a man and a woman to whom you can both turn to with questions and who will hold you accountable. The importance of having a mentor couple cannot be overstated or underestimated. They ask the tough questions and provide another safety net.

We have had a number of mentor couples and accountability partners over the years, and they will always be cherished for the investment they made in our marriage. With my accountability partner, I know that he will ask me certain questions regarding my walk with the Lord as well as my relationship with Debby. He will ask me about the things I do, the things I think about, and the places I go. He will ask if I have put myself in any compromising situations or if I am getting careless with relationships and friendships with co-workers or friends. By having a mentor couple, they will play the same role to some degree as an accountability partner, but they focus primarily on your relationship and your marriage.

If you have never had a mentor couple, seek out a couple from your circle of friends, or someone you trust, and ask them if they will work with you and your spouse in this manner. Give them permission to ask you the tough questions and begin a relationship with them. Regardless of where you are in your journey together as a couple, we all need accountability and we all need a more mature couple who has our best interests at heart and who have experienced life's challenges in their marriage as well.

In your search for a mentor couple, you want to select a couple that you can both relate to and people that you feel comfortable with. You

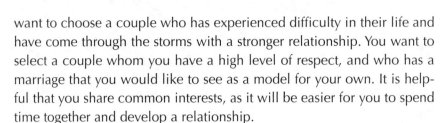

want to choose a couple who has experienced difficulty in their life and have come through the storms with a stronger relationship. You want to select a couple whom you have a high level of respect, and who has a marriage that you would like to see as a model for your own. It is helpful that you share common interests, as it will be easier for you to spend time together and develop a relationship.

The phrase "accountability partner" is used frequently in faith-based organizations, but you don't need to be a part of one of these organizations or churches to reap the benefits of being accountable to someone other than your spouse. It is a great tool to help you to make the right choices which will protect you and your marriage.

As you grow closer in your relationship with your wife and you develop your relationship with your mentor couple, you will want to reach out and help another couple. In this manner, you have a couple who is mentoring you and you are a mentor to a different couple. This couple will be your protégé. Don't wait until you think you have learned all you need to learn before you find a protégé. We never "arrive" or achieve the perfect marriage, and we are always learning and growing. Continue to grow your relationship on a daily basis so you avoid the hazards of your relationship becoming stale and slipping into a catatonic state of mediocrity. When you pour yourself into someone else, you help yourself at the same time. Zig Ziglar, a motivational speaker has said, "You can't help someone climb the mountain without getting closer to the top yourself."

When people approach you and notice that you have something that they want, something that is different in your marriage, you know that you need to be pouring yourself into a younger couple. As you look for a protégé couple, look for a couple where both the husband and the wife are willing to be coached, and who have the desire to learn and grow. Look for a couple who you believe is willing to pay the price of a mentoring relationship and who desires excellence in their relationship.

Biblical Perspective

As believers, we are called to be set apart from the world. When we are children of God, the Holy Spirit fills our lives and sanctifies us. That is, He sets apart us from the world. We are to live our lives differently; that means we are to act differently, talk differently, and have a different moral compass than the rest of the world. We are to be in the world but not of the world. (John 15:19).

We believe that part of this sanctification, or this being set apart and different, means that people should be able to look at the way we conduct ourselves and the way we live and see that there is something different. Others should be able to recognize that there is something unique about the choices we make and the way we treat people, particularly our lifelong mate. There should be a distinctive difference in the way we interact with our spouse and the priority we put on fulfilling our commitments to one another.

Unfortunately, most surveys and studies that we have seen show that the divorce rate among Christians is nearly the exact same rate as with non-Christians or non-religious couples. It seems that in general terms, the church is no better off than the rest of the world, when it comes to the sanctity of the marriage vows. How tragic, that the church has failed to set the example and exceed the standards set by the world. In an area that one might expect Bible-believing people to live beyond the level of mediocrity, it is apparent that there is no difference, according to the polls.

> It seems that in general terms, the church is no better off than the rest of the world, when it comes to the sanctity of the marriage vows.

The Barna Group found in its latest study that born again Christians who are not evangelical were indistinguishable from the national average on the matter of divorce with 33 percent having married and divorced at least once. Among all born again Christians, which includes evangelicals, the divorce figure is 32 percent, which is statistically identical to the 33 percent figure among non-born-again adults, the research group noted.[2]

When we talk about living a life that is set apart and different from the world, do not be mistaken. By no means are we suggesting that Christians or other faith-based couples or individuals are in any way superior to the rest of the world. Those of us who profess faith in Jesus Christ are just as guilty of sin as the non-believers. We are not saying that Christians

---

2 Study: Christian Divorce Rate Identical to National Average, by Audrey Barrick, Christian Post Reporter, April 04, 2008. http://www.christianpost.com/article/20080404/study-christian-divorce-rate-identical-to-national-average/index.html

are sinless, but if an individual is walking with God and is fully absorbed and abiding in His word, he or she is apt to sin less. The closer your relationship with the Lord is and the more time you spend in His Word, the more aware you become of the various temptations that are thrown your way and the more resistant you become. However, we are all born with a sin nature and we all succumb to the temptations of the flesh.

"By this all men will know that you are my disciples, if you love one another." John 13:35 (NIV) Jesus said that we are to live differently from the world, and that the world will know that we are His disciples by how we live our life. The love we have for one another will prove to the world that we are different, set apart and unique. Rather than blend in with the rest of the crowd, we are to love others and live our lives in a manner that points to the cross.

Being in a marriage of mediocrity is not my idea of being set apart from this world. When I think of being sanctified and set apart, I picture the type of life Christ would lead. We know that Jesus never married, but if He did marry while here on the earth, what do you think His marriage would look like? I think he would love sacrificially, give sacrificially, give of Himself with no expectation of reciprocation, and He would focus all of His affection, time, and attention on making His spouse feel as if she were the most important person in the world. Imagine for a moment what your marriage would look like if you did those things on a consistent basis.

If you loved your wife sacrificially, if you gave of yourself to your husband sacrificially, and if you spend all of your time and attention on each other, making him or her feel as if they were *the most important person in the world*, we can promise you that your marriage would be described as anything but mediocre! Write down one or two things you can do today that will begin to demonstrate to your spouse that he or she is the most important person in the world. You'll be glad you did.

Chapter 8

Forgiveness

"Forgiveness is choosing to love. It is the first skill of self-giving love."
~ Mohandas K. Gandhi

I imagine that the majority of you reading this chapter right now are expecting us to talk about how to forgive your spouse for infidelity. If you are a victim of infidelity, you may be thinking that your spouse walked out on you, betrayed your trust, and has slept with another man or woman, and that this chapter is dedicated to instructing you to forgive and forget. You may even be tempted to skip this chapter, because you don't want to forgive, or perhaps your marriage has not been affected by infidelity. Perhaps you don't think you should forgive, or maybe you just can't bring yourself to the point of forgiveness. Well, you're right, and you're wrong, and we hope you continue reading.

We will talk about how to forgive that act of betrayal, but, while infidelity doesn't affect all marriages, all couples wrestle with the need for forgiveness in their relationship. So, before we focus on infidelity, we need to deal with the more fundamental act of forgiveness and just what it means to forgive.

We all deal with disappointments and things that our spouse either does or says that hurts us. Even in the best of relationships, there are times when we offend or hurt our loved ones and we need to ask for their forgiveness. After all, we are by nature, selfish and stingy people who look out for ourselves first and foremost, regardless of how it affects other people. It's this "me first" attitude that often causes us to short-change our spouse and focus on meeting our own needs rather than focusing on their needs. This leads to unmet expectations and disappointment.

When your spouse comes to you and says that he or she is sorry for something they have done or said, how do you respond? Do you immediately accept their apology and move on with life, or do you press them for reasons as to why they did or said what they did?

Oftentimes the reason behind an offense really isn't that important. People spend far too much time trying to find out why something was done or said, rather than focusing on how to get past the hurt and the pain. What's important is that the offending party comes to realize that what was done or said was hurtful and wrong, and they need to come to a point of asking for forgiveness.

> An amazing marriage consists of complete forgiveness and restoration in your relationship for all the hurts and wrongdoing.

When someone asks for forgiveness, they are demonstrating a change in their attitude. If we, the hurt or offended one, refuse to accept that apology and we harbor bad feelings for our spouse, we are perpetuating the problem and potentially causing even more suffering than what was caused by the initial offense.

We need to come to an understanding or realization that our relationship is far more valuable and important than the words or actions that wounded our pride, let us down, or in some other way caused us to feel insignificant. We encourage you to accept that change of heart and apology, if it is sincere, and move beyond the offense. Begin to rebuild the relationship and move forward. As difficult as it may seem at the time, your attitude and feelings can change and you will see your spouse in a better light after forgiveness has taken place.

If you hang on to the offense and refuse to fully forgive, which many of us often do, it can eat away at you and lead to emotional and even physical distress. Sometimes, you may even tell your spouse that you forgive them, yet at a later date and time of your choosing, you bring up the offense in an accusatory manner. When you do this, you really haven't truly and completely forgiven them. You may try and smooth things over for a period of time; but if you don't completely forgive one another, you delay the restoration process.

You need to fully reconcile, which means to restore harmony between two people. An amazing marriage consists of complete forgiveness and restoration in your relationship for all the hurts and wrongdoing. If you want an amazing marriage, you need to realize the importance of this reconciliation and clear up disagreements and hurts as soon as possible.

We have talked to a number of couples over the past few years as we have prepared to write this book, and we have found that one of the challenges many couples face is that of complete forgiveness. It is easy to forgive your spouse after a disagreement or after something hurtful has been said, but if you file that comment or act away in your memory for future use against your spouse, you have not truly forgiven them.

A good example comes from early in our own marriage. We would be having one of our quarterly fights and one of us would recall small things that the other had done or said since our last fight, as if to heap more coals on the fire of the argument. We were both guilty of that at times. It was as if we would strengthen our position in the current argument by bringing out all the previous bad deeds of the other and thereby justify our own actions or words. We would bring a gallon of gasoline to a bonfire rather than marshmallows and chocolate.

It was a terrible tactic, but one that we really didn't understand the consequences of for a number of years. When we realized that we had a problem with complete forgiveness, we were able to talk through it and learn how to leave past hurts where they belong, in the past. When you and your spouse have a disagreement, you most likely have enough things to worry about and enough to resolve with your current issue, without bringing up old hurts that you've already worked through.

One other major lesson I needed to learn was how to listen. That was a tough lesson, as I always thought I was a pretty good listener. Boy, was I wrong about that! I needed to learn to give Debby the freedom to talk about anything she wanted, and to just listen. No comments, no interruptions, and certainly no sarcasm or defensive attitude. This principle, of course, needs to be practiced by both spouses, not just the husband. Wives, be sensitive to what your husband chooses to say and give him the same respect you desire. Regardless of what his actions may show you, your husband is desperate for your attention and acceptance. You are the most important sounding board your husband has. He gains confidence from his relationship with you and he can then go out into the world with confidence in his dealings with others.

Absence of Trust

If there is an absence of trust, you need to rebuild the trust you once shared and reestablish your trustworthiness. This will undoubtedly be a long and tiresome process, but one that is fundamental to your relationship. If you were the offending party and you need to reestablish his or her trust in you, you will most likely try and rush the process. You may

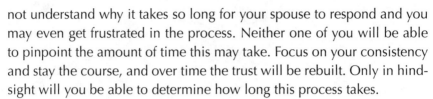

not understand why it takes so long for your spouse to respond and you may even get frustrated in the process. Neither one of you will be able to pinpoint the amount of time this may take. Focus on your consistency and stay the course, and over time the trust will be rebuilt. Only in hindsight will you be able to determine how long this process takes.

Don't give up and don't let up. Reestablishing trust is definitely worth the time you will invest. Like any good investment, you need to be in it for the long haul. There is no short-term process for rebuilding trust. Rebuilding trust is not like a get-rich-quick scheme that promises an immediate payoff. It takes purpose, patience, focus, and an incredible amount of effort.

If infidelity is the cause of the absence of trust, you can still save your marriage if you work at it. Assuming that your spouse has confessed the infidelity, has turned away from the extramarital affair, has put an end to the infidelity, and wants to work toward restoration, you will need to reestablish the trust that has been lost. Trust is a key ingredient in your relationship, much like flour in a cake recipe. Without trust, there can be no restoration to the relationship and no growth. Without flour in your cake batter, all you have is sweetened egg whites. You might say that trust is the foundation upon which your relationship is built.

Infidelity

One of the most difficult challenges to marriages today is an affair—a sexual relationship, a passionate physical encounter, or an emotional connection with someone other than your spouse. There are many things one may say or do to hurt a spouse that can be easily forgiven, but once the trust is broken by an emotional or sexual relationship that is forged with another, the results are usually devastating.

The sexual aspect of marriage is the most coveted and restricted privilege a married couple shares. It's the special bond that can only be found between a husband and wife and it is sacred to the relationship. The sexual relationship the two of you share cannot be duplicated in its original form, though it can be forged. Much like a counterfeit twenty dollar bill; it may look similar and feel similar, but there is no true value to the counterfeit. Similarly, only the original relationship has lasting value.

When the sexual relationship is violated and another is allowed to enter the equation, everything changes. It is no longer just a husband who fails to help with the kids or doesn't do work around the house. It is no longer simply a wife who says hurtful things or doesn't respect her husband. These things can be handled and overcome, they can be talked about and worked through—and they can be forgiven. However, infidelity hurts like nothing else hurts and has far more devastating effects on the marriage relationship. Most people can't get past this land mine like they can get over other things because of the vastly intimate aspect of infidelity.

Sex is obviously the most intimate relationship we can have with someone. When we enter a marriage commitment, we pledge our fidelity and faithfulness to the one we marry. Among the vows we exchange, the one that most people view as the most crucial and critical is the pledge of giving of ourselves physically to each other, and only to each other. It is a unique relationship that we don't have with others and it is an intimately personal relationship. When that vow is broken, and we allow another to enter into our most intimate and personal space, we violate the commitment we have made to one another and it is extremely hard to overcome a violation of trust to that degree.

I have often found this to be interesting: single people who aren't of the conviction that sex should be reserved only for married couples still have a sense of loyalty and commitment to the one they are with. A man may be dating a woman and be sexually active with her; yet, if she were to have sex with another man, their relationship would most likely be over.

Add the covenant of marriage, and the devastating result of a cheating spouse is even greater. We are certainly not advocating it, but I have found that most individuals morally comfortable with polygamous relations typically have only one partner at a time and value loyalty and commitment. He or she remains loyal and true to their partner, until that relationship ends and they find another partner.

The point is simple: sex is an intimate and personal relationship intended to be shared by two people exclusively. Regardless of morality or religious beliefs, the vast majority of people engage in monogamous sexual relationships. Our belief is that sex should be shared exclusively between a man and a woman within the bonds of a marriage covenant. The consequences of infidelity can be staggering.

In the electronic environment we live in, we are bombarded hundreds of times a day with sexually suggestive ads, references, and innuendos.

Cars, beverages, electronics, and almost everything advertised on television and in magazines imply a sexual connection or are sexually suggestive. There is a particular mall-based clothing store that Debby refuses to shop in because the majority of their ads are extremely seductive and sexually suggestive. We live in a sexually charged environment and it is no wonder that couples struggle with sexual temptation.

Pornography is readily available to anyone with an Internet connection or at your local convenience store and many marriages are in dire straights due to the over-abundance and easy access to pornography. Oftentimes a relationship may be strained and the sex all but ceases to exist, and the husband turns to pornography as an alternative.

When his wife discovers the websites he has been visiting or finds magazines hidden away, she begins to have doubts and fears. These fears can compound and grow, potentially creating more and even bigger problems than the couple was facing initially. The wife may think that she is no longer attractive to her husband and she is led to believe, in many cases, that he is having an affair. This begins a chain-reaction of thoughts and actions that typically have damaging consequences.

If you are facing the potential of a cheating spouse, you may be wondering what you can do and where your relationship will go from here. You may be asking yourself if you still have a future together with your spouse. How can you get beyond the thoughts of your spouse with another, and how could you possibly get over the hurt? These are just a few of the many questions that people find themselves facing on a daily basis.

Dr. James Dobson has written an excellent book, *Tough Love*, that helps victims of infidelity cope with their feelings and work through what may be the fiercest storm an individual could face. No one ever wants to discover that their loved one has found another lover, and this book outlines steps one could take to begin to mend the heart and repair the damage. If your spouse has had an affair, or you think he or she is engaged in an affair currently and you want to save your marriage, it is a must-read that we highly recommend.

You may be wondering how you could ever get beyond the thought of your lover with another man or woman and how your relationship could be restored to what it once was. Without writing an entire book on the subject of restoration, as Dr. Dobson has done, let us suggest four key elements we have found in our own lives to be critical in regaining or reestablishing trust. These four elements are Time, Commitment, Accountability, and Consistency.

Time

There is no substitution for time when it comes to reestablishing trust. This will be a long and hard process, for both of you. Unfortunately, the thoughts of the indiscretion will never completely go away. Even after time has gone by and you think your relationship is on the road to recovery, there will be times when you have mental flashbacks. Something you encounter throughout your day may trigger a thought and your mind is right back to the time of the affair. It could be something as simple as a name, a city, or some other piece of information that acts as a reminder, even years later. Whether you are the offender or the victim, this may affect you in a similar fashion.

The thoughts may never go away, but we can encourage you and tell you that they will be dulled by time. The sharp cutting edge of the pain will be washed away over time, similar to the erosion of rocks by the ocean tides. Over time, the memories will become less and less painful and you will be able to refocus your thoughts. They will still surface, and you will be reminded from time to time, but the memories will fade and as time passes you will recall them less often.

Time is necessary for both of you. Time is necessary for you as the victim of the infidelity, as you need to work through the memories of the pain. Time is also necessary for the offending spouse, as he or she will need to spend an inordinate amount of time in winning back your trust.

This can be a trying period, where one or both of you may be tempted to give up and file for divorce, thinking it's just not worth the effort. It is worth it. You are worth it. Your relationship is worth it. Think about it this way: if there is no cost involved, would your relationship really be worth having or saving? There are truly very few things in life that are absolutely free and yet are worth having.

Restoring your relationship will be costly and, at times, may even seem out of reach, but it is worth it in the long run. You or your spouse may not initially think that it is worth paying the price, but those are usually the times when you are close to making a breakthrough and victory is within reach. You may not understand how close you are to restoring your relationship to its fullest, and if you drop out of the fight you will never know.

Here's an encouraging thought: The memory you have of a cheating spouse may be a constant reminder of the devastation the affair caused, and that memory may be the driving factor in helping you to resist temptation yourself at some point. We need to be honest with ourselves. We are all tempted in some way at various points in our marriage. The degree of temptation will certainly vary, but we are all tempted; how we deal with that temptation is crucial.

Merely being attracted to someone is not the problem and you cannot live your life in such a bubble of protection that you never encounter someone who sparks an interest in you, if only momentarily. The problem is not the initial attraction or the first look, but the potential problems lie with what you do with that attraction. Do you turn back for a second, third, or even forth look?

We believe that you are only fooling yourself if you believe that neither you nor your spouse will ever be attracted to someone else. We all need to recognize that this will happen at some point in the marriage and most likely more than once. You and your spouse owe it to one another to have safety nets in place to guard your hearts and not allow anyone else into your marriage.

The initial attraction doesn't become a problem until it develops into lustful desires. If you find yourself thinking about and perhaps even fantasizing about that individual, then you have crossed the line. If you go out of your way to create a chance encounter at the coffee shop or the grocery store, you are adding fuel to the fire of temptation and you have crossed the line. The fires of temptation, if fed even a little kindling, can ignite into a raging firestorm with little or no warning. What may seem to be innocent contact, could lead to a devastating escalation of desire.

If you find yourself at this point, even now, acknowledge it for what it is and take steps to guard your heart. Talk to your spouse openly and honestly and ask him or her to help you to do whatever it takes to avoid that individual. We realize this can be a very scary revelation to your spouse; however, the benefits of having your spouse help you resist temptation far outweigh any negative impact from your spouse. Step out in boldness and be honest with one another; you will not regret it and your spouse will thank you for your honesty. Remember, the initial attraction is not wrong; it is the pursuit of that attraction which may be fatal.

A pastor I know told me recently that there was a particular woman in his congregation that seemed to be attracted to him, and through her words and actions he knew that she was interested in him. To protect himself, he openly discussed this with his wife and his elders, and asked the elders of the church to intervene in any conversation he had with this woman.

If she approached him before or after a church service, his standing orders were to break in on the conversation and pull him away, so there was never an opportunity for her to engage him in an extended conversation or get the wrong impression that he wanted to spend time with her. The Bible clearly warns Christians to "avoid all appearance of evil," and this pastor wanted to be certain that no one saw him with this woman or, worse, started to spread rumors about them. He was acting in a very appropriate manner to protect his marriage, as well as the reputations of both himself and this woman.

It has been said that time has a way of healing all hurts. It won't take the memories away completely, but it will certainly help you to cope with the hurt and help you restore your relationship. Additionally, you may see someone who catches your eye or is attractive to you in some way, and as you recall the devastating blow your marriage took because your spouse was unfaithful, it may be a reminder and a deterrent to keep you from pursuing any inappropriate contact with that individual. It may actually be a good thing that you don't fully forget the pain you suffered in the past, as it can help keep you accountable and help you avoid making a similar mistake.

Commitment

The amount of pain that is caused by infidelity far surpasses that of your common disagreement or fight. The sense of disloyalty, breach of trust, lack of commitment, and many other thoughts go through the mind of the victim, and the cheating spouse often does not comprehend or appreciate the full extent or impact of their actions. To restore trust in your relationship, both parties need to demonstrate commitment to one another and a commitment toward reconciliation of the relationship.

It is not uncommon for the victimized spouse to feel as if the commitment from his or her spouse is questionable, given the fact that trust has already been broken and there may be a history of broken commitments.

In the initial stages, you need to be committed to the process of restoration, regardless of what your spouse may do or say. You need to be committed to doing everything you can throughout this process, but without smothering your spouse or forcing reconciliation.

Anybody who feels pushed into reconciliation simply to pacify his or her spouse won't be in it for the long haul and true reconciliation will not happen. If there is not a change in the heart, true confession, sincere repentance, and a desire for reconciliation, it will only result in additional failure and disappointment.

As we have said, this process may take a considerable amount of time, perhaps even years, and you may be tempted to throw in the towel of defeat and just walk away. You need to know that the process of reconciliation and complete forgiveness is a long and hard journey, and that there are disappointments along the way.

You may feel as if you want more reassurance from your spouse, more acceptance from your spouse, or perhaps even a higher level of accountability than you had previously. You may feel that the restoration process is not moving along quickly enough, or you may encounter other obstacles. If you are committed to the process of reconciliation, you will be better equipped to fight off doubts, fears, and a myriad of distractions—and stay the course.

It comes down to a matter of your will. Do you love your spouse enough to stay committed to the process of restoration, regardless of how tough the road may be and how long the journey?

Accountability

Accountability is one of the biggest components of rebuilding trust. If you are the one who has broken the marriage commitment and you are trying to reestablish the trust that your husband or wife had in you, you need to be more than fully committed to the process in everything you do. You cannot go about this half-heartedly nor can you expect immediate results.

It is imperative that you be accountable to your spouse in every aspect of your life. This includes where you go, when you go, and when you return. Who you see, who you talk to, and who you e-mail. Where you have lunch, where you shop, and how you spend both your time and money. Essentially, your life will need to be an open book, without reservation and without secrets. Your e-mail passwords must be shared with your spouse and access to any voice messaging you have for both home and work should be available. In addition, your spouse needs to have full access to your cell phone records, including any text messaging history. In today's high-tech environment, there are numerous methods of communication available and you need to be fully accountable in all areas. We encourage this type of accountability, even without the added dimension of working through infidelity. Perhaps this level of accountability will help to protect you and your marriage.

In order to fully establish accountability, you need to demonstrate openness and transparency in all things. If you withhold any information, such as who you have contact with throughout your day and who you interact with, it may naturally lead to your spouse questioning your actions, your motives, and your commitment to the process. When you volunteer this information rather than waiting to be questioned, you demonstrate your willingness to be held accountable and your willingness to pursue complete reconciliation.

If you are trying to win your spouse back, there may be times you feel as if there is nothing you can do without either first getting permission from your spouse or giving complete details when you return. This is actually part of the price you must pay for restoration. You need to be completely transparent and forthright as you account for your time. You may feel that this level of scrutiny and accountability is not necessary, but keep in mind that you are the one who initially broke the covenant relationship and it is you who needs to reestablish the trust. That, my friend, means you need to be patient and understanding, for as long as it takes.

As much as you may want to, you cannot blame your spouse for asking questions. This is not their fault nor is it something he or she brought upon you. Do not think that your spouse is unjustified in knowing your whereabouts. Being where you say you will be, and being home when you say you will be home will go a long way in helping you rebuild trust. Do not be surprised if your spouse asks you to account for the mileage in your car or asks questions if you are late. This is all part of the process.

Keep in mind that what your spouse needs right now more than anything else is reassurance. He or she needs reassurance that you love them, reassurance that you are repentant and are committed to rebuilding your relationship, and reassurance that you are being completely honest. The more you are accountable in every aspect of your life, the more likely it will be that your spouse recognizes your efforts toward reconciliation and begins to believe in you and in your marriage again.

Nothing may be more important to your spouse than the fact that you are accountable in all ways. This demonstrates your willingness to move forward and recommit yourself to your spouse and to your relationship. This is a long process that may take weeks, months, or perhaps longer, depending on the history of trust, or breach of trust, that you have in your marriage. This process requires you to make good choices, be accountable in all things, and stay the course.

Consistency

As you restore your relationship and rebuild trust, it is essential that you are consistent. When you are consistent in your efforts to rebuild trust and you are dependable, this sends a strong message to your spouse that you are truly committed to your relationship and committed to him or her. There are so many different emotions your spouse is feeling during this process and the fact that you are consistently demonstrating love and accountability means more than you can appreciate and understand.

When time is invested and commitments are made and followed up on, you are off to a good start. When accountability becomes a priority and all of these things are done with consistency, the relationship is on the path toward healing and restoration. Your spouse will have a level of expectation that is developed as you go through this process and one thing that will add to your credibility is your ability to be consistent. Don't expect immediate resolution, but be encouraged and know that the efforts you are making will result in restoration.

Forgiveness Begins with a Conscious Decision

Just as you need to make a conscious effort to love your spouse on a daily basis, the act of forgiveness begins with a conscious decision to forgive. You need to want to forgive, and you need to make the choice to forgive. You need to be able to completely release your spouse from the hurt and pain he or she has caused, and move toward complete forgiveness. It may take a week, a month, a year, or perhaps several years, but the benefits and blessings you will receive for your efforts will far outweigh the difficulty it took to get there.

118

For the spouse who has had to face the fact that his or her marriage partner has cheated on them, it is a long and hard road toward recovery. However, in many cases, infidelity can be overcome, the problems of the past can be forgiven, and a new relationship can be established. Forgiveness basically comes down to a choice: do you want to forgive and forge ahead in your marriage, truly living out the for-better-or-for-worse vow, or do you want to end the relationship and all you have built your life around? It is not fair that you have to make this choice and it is certainly a hard process, but couples all over the world are faced with this choice.

There is a freedom you will experience when you can finally release someone from the pain they have inflicted when you choose to completely forgive them. People often tend to lie awake at night trying to unpack the past hurts and hang on to a word or a deed that was done, when what they really need to do is let go of that hurt and move on. If the betrayal has been confessed and if repentance has been demonstrated, then you have to choose whether or not you will release your spouse from the burden of guilt and shame.

If these things have been demonstrated, we encourage you to forgive. Forgive your spouse and forgive completely. Choose to be different and choose to stay married! The forgiveness you have to offer can elevate your marriage and take your relationship to new levels you never thought possible. The relationship Debby and I developed over the years is by far stronger and deeper than we ever imagined and we owe it in part to the trials we faced together and the battles we fought to save our marriage. We fought side by side to keep our marriage together under some of the harshest of conditions and we are fully committed to one another, regardless of the circumstances we may find ourselves in. We would never have chosen to face the infidelity that we have had to work through in our marriage, but we were able to overcome that, among many other things, and have drawn closer to one another in the process.

Revenge—The Inappropriate Response

If a husband or wife has an affair, it is not uncommon at some point for the spouse to consider the possibility of responding in kind—in other words, to have an affair of their own, as if in some way they are getting back at their cheating spouse. They may try to justify their actions and say they are just leveling the playing field.

You may be so devastated when you discover the news of your husband or wife's infidelity that your first reaction is to respond in an irrational manner. You may try to bury your pain and attempt to replace the hurt with the comfort of someone else. You may have a friend of the opposite sex with whom you choose to confide in, and in the process you may be unknowingly drawn into an inappropriate relationship yourself while you are trying to deal with the cheating spouse.

Keep in mind that failure is never fatal and failure is never final.

Be wary of these types of situations and remain on guard. You should always confide in a same-gender friend to avoid the possibility of developing reliance on someone else for emotional support, which may develop into something far greater than you ever imagined or intended. Revenge will never heal the pain and will not get you any closer to restoration.

Keep in mind that failure is never fatal and failure is never final. We all make mistakes, say things we regret, and, on occasion, do stupid things. We're human, and it is our nature to be self-serving. If you can learn from your failures and apply those lessons in your life, you can experience life to the fullest. You can grow beyond your failures and live a productive life with strong relationships.

When you understand that you need forgiveness as much as others who may have failed you, you can offer the complete forgiveness that is necessary and move beyond the hurt and the pain. If you choose to, you can offer forgiveness and/or receive forgiveness, and restore your relationship, allowing you to defeat failure and build your marriage into the growing and thriving marriage that you desire.

Our marriage is a prime example of a marriage that has survived the impact of infidelity and has come out on the other side not only stronger but with a higher level of commitment to one another and to our marriage. If your marriage has been rocked by infidelity, our desire is that you, too, make a serious effort toward forgiveness and restoration and establish a renewed commitment toward one another. Don't allow a moment of weakness to destroy the dreams and plans you made with one another. Instead, turn your mistakes and failures into victory. Use these experiences to strengthen your commitment to one another as you elevate your relationship into an amazing marriage.

Biblical Perspective

When we think of the greatest people in the Bible, we cannot complete a Top 10 list of biblical heroes without including King David. He was anointed king as a young boy and in 1 Sam 13:14 is called a "man after God's own heart." Unfortunately for David, the thing he is most often remembered for, besides his victory over Goliath, is his adulterous encounter with Bathsheba and the murder of her husband Uriah to cover up his sin.

When Nathan confronts David with his sin, David cries out to God for forgiveness. He asks for mercy, acknowledges his sin, repents, and turns from his sin. Psalm 51:10 says, "Create in me a clean heart, O God; and renew a right spirit within me." David recognized his need for forgiveness and cleansing, and asked God to renew his mind. David knew what he did was terrible in the sight of God and he knew that he needed to seek forgiveness.

I think we can all agree that adultery and murder are two very serious offenses, but if God can forgive David and then use him for His glory and purpose, surely God can forgive you and me for our trespasses and sins as well. In God's economy, all sin, regardless of it's severity, leads to separation from God and is worthy of punishment. In spite of our weakness and sinful nature, we can look to Him for the power of complete forgiveness. For example, we can sin in our minds (1 John 3:15), with our words (Matthew 5:22), and with our actions (Genesis 3:16–17); and all three of these types of sin are an abomination to the Lord. However, if we ask Him to forgive us, we have redemption through His blood (Ephesians 1:7). Acts 13:38 assures us that through Jesus we can receive forgiveness of sin.

David goes on a few verses later in Psalm 51 to ask God to restore the joy of His salvation. Are you aware that God can restore you and your relationship, regardless of what you may have done? As terrible as infidelity is, God is bigger than that and any other sin we may commit. He is capable and willing to forgive us of all our trespasses and sins, and according to I John 1:9, He promises to "cleanse us from all unrighteousness" (NKJV).

He wants to forgive you, if you'll only ask Him. He allowed His Son to die to pay the penalty of your sin and for mine, and He truly wants to forgive you. If your spouse had an affair, Jesus wants to forgive him or her and restore your relationship. He desires to give you back the joy you once knew. He desires to reestablish the harmony and restore the joy in your marriage. His desire for you is to develop a callous over the injury and renew your relationship both with Him and with your spouse.

If God can and will forgive, you must also forgive yourself and others. Do you have a tendency to hang on to certain things and not let them go? Has someone, perhaps your spouse, done something to you that you just can't forgive? Maybe it isn't something as painful as infidelity, but it has hurt you in a way that you will not soon forget. Perhaps you are unable to forgive yourself for things you know you have done.

Remember that Christ paid the penalty *once and for all*. He forgives and He forgets. He says He has cast our sin as far as the east is from the west (Psalm 103:12), so if *He* can let it go, why can't you? If you continue to harbor thoughts and feelings and if you refuse to forgive someone, it will eat away at you and you may not be able to enjoy all that God intends for you. You may not be able to restore the relationship with the one who has offended you, and your other relationships may suffer as well. Colossians 3:13 says, "Bear with each other and forgive whatever grievances you may have against one another. Forgive as the Lord forgave you."(NIV)

Jesus didn't die to pay a partial payment for our sin; He died to pay the debt in full. There is nothing we can do that He can't forgive. We can have complete forgiveness through the cross and we can have our relationship restored to the fullest (Hebrews 8:12). He desires a relationship with us and has demonstrated that when He willingly gave up His life that we may have life. The only way we can have the abundant life that He promises is if we seek and receive the complete forgiveness of the cross.

When it comes to retaliation, or revenge, don't allow these thoughts to enter your mind. Revenge may be something you think of as a way of striking back and causing your spouse to feel some of the pain you felt. You may even get spiritual in your defense, because after all, the Bible does say eye for an eye, doesn't it?

That one biblical quotation may be well known by many, but the context is not as well known. The eye-for-an-eye response was the practice under the Jewish Law in the Old Testament, and can be found in Exodus, Leviticus, and Deuteronomy.

However, when the law was abolished with Jesus Christ and the dispensation of grace was ushered in, Jesus says, ". . . do not resist an evil person and turn the other cheek." (Matt. 5:39) No longer are we to retaliate when someone attacks us and pluck out an eye or cut off a hand. Can you imagine? That is obviously a practice that would not be tolerated under our current legal system. In similar manner, we are not to retaliate and try to hurt our spouse and have an affair of our own simply because of a mistake they made.

Applying the eye-for-an-eye response is an impulsive reaction someone may use to hurt their spouse, but it is a completely irrational and erroneous response. John C. Maxwell says that, "hurting people hurt people," and we need to be careful not to fall for the temptation to retaliate in this manner.

God is all about reconciliation and forgiveness. His desire is for you and I to live in harmony with Him and with others, and because of His unwavering love for us, we can be assured that failure is not fatal and failure is not final. Write this on your bathroom mirror, or somewhere else so that you will be reminded of it on a daily basis: Failure is Not Fatal and Failure is Not Final. We have all sinned and we have all failed, yet through His forgiveness we can put our failures behind us and live victoriously in Christ. We read in 1 Corinthians 15:57, "But thanks be to God! He gives us the victory through our Lord Jesus Christ." (NIV) Practice forgiveness. Make allowance for each other's faults, and forgive anyone who offends you. Remember, the Lord forgave you, so you must forgive others. (Colossians 3:13)

Recently I heard a preacher say that you discover your theology at midnight. He went on to say that we need to work out our theology, or decide what we truly believe, prior to facing trials. It's not until we are facing a major crisis in our life that we discover who we really are, what we believe, and how we will respond to difficult circumstances.

In Acts chapter 16, Paul and Silas were imprisoned for preaching the Gospel. The text tells us that they were not just regular prisoners, but that they were bound, hand and foot, and they were in the inner cell. This tells me that the Roman guards were seriously concerned that these two prisoners might escape and that they were high-profile prisoners.

As midnight approached, Paul and Silas were praying and singing. Can you imagine that? In the midst of the worst crisis you have faced, you pray and sing? Unfortunately, I must admit that I couldn't always do this.

As the text continues (Acts 16: 26–28), we read about an earthquake that destroys the prison. The quake is strong enough to knock down the walls and loosen the chains holding the prisoners. When the prison guard sees this, he draws his sword to kill himself rather than face his superiors with the news that he allowed the prisoners to escape.

Paul and Silas cry out to the guard and assure him that they and all the prisoners are still there (they didn't escape). Upon hearing this, the guard is so overcome with emotion and he recognizes that he wants what these two prisoners have: faith in a higher being. The guard falls to his knees and asks, "Sirs, what must I do to be saved?" What follows, of course, is one of the most quoted verses in the entire Bible, Acts 16:31, "They replied, 'Believe in the Lord Jesus and you will be saved, along with everyone in your household.'"

Now, you may be asking yourself, what does this have to do with marriage? How can we apply the story of two prisoners to the relationship between a man and a woman? Paul and Silas prayed and they sang in the midst of turmoil. They knew, that no matter the depth of their despair and problems they could trust God and have faith that He would see them through. Whatever the outcome, they had already determined in their hearts that they would praise God. Can you say that in your marriage? When things look the darkest and you are both in the midst of a storm, will you and your spouse be faithful enough to pray and sing? Are you grounded enough in your faith to trust Him with all things, and give praise? (Job 1:21)

In reading the text, I conclude that Paul and Silas were unified. They didn't complain and they didn't blame one another. We need to follow their example and be in unity with our spouse. You need to have common goals and an agreement, in advance, as to how you will handle adversity. You must also accept the fact that this will all be theory until you are faced with the trial, or faced with reality. If you and your spouse discuss potential obstacles before they arise and you decide on a course of action, you have a much higher chance of making the right decisions when faced with adversity and you will have a much higher rate of success. This is what Debby and I did when we agreed that divorce is not an option.

Having dialogue and agreeing on common goals when things are good and the sailing is smooth helps to prepare you to face the unknown future. Having established certain mutual goals has allowed us to endure a myriad of storms in our marriage, including infidelity, and has allowed us to pray and sing through both the good times and rough times alike.

Having conversations and role playing situations will prepare you to respond to a situation rather than to react to one. A response is a measured and premeditated plan of action, while a reaction is impulsive and often thoughtless. You can think of it as having an emergency evacuation plan set in place.

When our relationship was nearly shattered due to infidelity (within the first six months of our young marriage), it would have been so easy for us to give up and walk away. It not only would have been easy, it would have been biblically acceptable to God if we allowed the result of poor choices to destroy what we were building.

Only by the grace of God and our commitment to one another were we able to trust that God would carry us through the storm and that He would restore our relationship. Like Paul and Silas who refused to escape when given the opportunity, we stood our ground, faced our trials, and refused to escape. Like Paul and Silas, we discovered our theology at midnight and found that it was sufficient because we had dared to agree on common goals prior to facing the storms of life. We had previously decided that divorce is not an option, so we were forced to find another way through our trials, rather than take the easy escape route and avoid them altogether.

This certainly isn't to say that it was an easy or quick fix. The pain we both suffered as a result stayed with us for a very long time, and it was an incredible and difficult journey to restore trust and confidence. We relied upon God's complete grace and the forgiveness He promised in Philippians 1:6, ". . . being confident of this, that he who began a good work in you will carry it on to completion until the day of Christ Jesus." (NIV)

We knew it wasn't God's plan for us to end our marriage so quickly and we also knew that He had great things in store for us. It was more difficult than we can express, but we knew that our love was meant to be eternal, and that anything worth having is worth fighting for.

Now, over twenty years later, we are able to reflect on mistakes we have made along the way and encourage you, our readers, that God does have a plan and a purpose for your life. Remember the words of Jeremiah 29:11: "'For I know the plans I have for you,' says the LORD. 'They are plans for good and not for disaster, to give you a future and a hope.'"

He wants you to fulfill His plans and He wants you to be blessed. We can look back now and see that God is able to use this near tragedy in our lives to encourage others to hang on to one another and find a way to resolve whatever is trying to tear their marriage apart. Whether it is infidelity, betrayal, dishonesty, abuse, or any number of things that you face in your relationship, He has a plan for good for your life and He is standing nearby, waiting for you to call out to Him and to cast all your cares at the cross. Leave your burdens with Him, and allow Him to restore your joy and harmony. He loves you, and promises to carry you through.

Chapter 9

Your Marriage Under Attack

"Love is much like a wild rose, beautiful and calm, but willing to draw blood in its defense." ~ Mark Overby

Life is distracting. We are all extremely busy and we often fill our lives with frivolous distractions to avoid addressing the core issues we are facing. There are many ways marriages today are under attack, besides the obvious one of infidelity. We know that infidelity can have disastrous consequences, but we want to address other ways in which your marriage can be attacked as well.

Over-Commitment of Time

Imagine this: It's 5:00 PM and you are rushing to leave your office on time for the commute home. Along the way, your Blackberry chimes in with a Task Reminder and you see that you forgot the monthly meeting for the school booster club, which starts at 7 PM tonight. You are frantic because you forgot about the report you volunteered to prepare for this meeting and you have absolutely no idea how you will get through the meeting without it, let alone survive through dinner when you need to tell your wife that you have to attend this meeting.

As you pull into your driveway, your cell phone rings and your son's baseball coach asks you if you can run practice tomorrow night because he needs to attend a school concert that his daughter is playing in. You readily agree to coach the practice, and then it dawns on you as you hang up the phone that your daughter has a piano recital at 7:30 tomorrow night too.

As you throw your presentation together for tonight's meeting, you see forty-two unanswered e-mails in your inbox, and the bills still need to be paid—the bills that were due last week. You wonder when you will

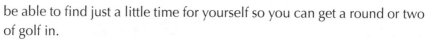

be able to find just a little time for yourself so you can get a round or two of golf in.

Sound familiar? Perhaps the actual events are different for you, but most of us find ourselves over-committed. Between the school, sports, volunteer positions, church, the activities we enjoy with our friends and co-workers, and, of course, the time we spend on our careers, it is very easy to be over-extended.

When this happens, the time you have available to spend with your spouse and family is greatly reduced. When you spend an inordinate amount of time volunteering in organizations, or even a considerable amount of time working, it is not uncommon for this to take a toll on relationships.

When you become so over-committed outside the home that your spouse begins to think you are intentionally away from home, you have a massive problem on your hands that will demand an immediate remedy. This over-commitment has potential to negatively impact your spouse and your marriage. It's time to reevaluate priorities, activities, volunteer positions, and maybe even your work schedule, if possible. Your spouse may not communicate their thoughts to you, but if you conclude that they may be thinking this then it is imperative that you talk about it immediately.

Let your spouse know that you realize you are over-extended and reassure them that this was not intentional and you will do whatever you can to scale back and begin spending more time at home. Assure him or her that you will make an intentional effort to begin to invest more time in your relationship, and then follow that discussion up with immediate action.

I have recently come to the conclusion that I was over-extended myself. As I was planning out my monthly schedule, I realized that I have far too many meetings and appointments that occupy my time, and I thought it would be great if I could just spend a quiet night at home on occasion. Besides being a husband and a dad, I have a full-time job. I was the president of the gymnastics booster club for one of my daughters, the treasurer of the high school booster club, and the treasurer of a local para-church organization. In addition to that, Debby and I serve on a support team for a local missionary, which requires involvement in local church youth clubs. Wow. My head spins just thinking of all that!

Since coming to the conclusion that I was over-extended, I began to take immediate steps to free myself up from the majority of those commitments. I have already resigned from one of the treasurer positions and have submitted my resignation notice from the other treasurer position and the president position, both effective the end of the current annual commitment. By the time this book finds itself in your hands, I will be completely free of all of these extra-curricular responsibilities.

What will I do with all this time on my hands? Love my wife and kids! I know these decisions will show Debby that our marriage and family are my top priorities. I realize that even though I've gotten over-extended in the past, it is definitely worth the effort to scale back and reinvest in our relationship.

When I told Debby that I was going to step away from all of these responsibilities, she encouraged me to do so if that is what I felt I needed to do, but also said that she felt I was doing a good job balancing these responsibilities and she hasn't felt as if her or the kids were being short-changed as far as my time is concerned. She was supportive of my involvement outside the home because I have been careful to plan meetings and appointments around our home schedule and I have kept her informed of my activities. If you prioritize correctly, your efforts will be acknowledged and rewarded.

If you are an organized person and you are able to compartmentalize the different responsibilities you have, you may be able to pull off the multiple volunteer positions successfully, but let us encourage you to learn to say no more often. It seems as if the more involved our kids are in school activities, sports, or church, the more often these organizations ask us to volunteer our time. Before you know it, you will have so many commitments you will become stretched thin and no longer be as effective in all areas.

The need for volunteers in schools, sports, and communities will always be abundant. Organizations asking you and me to volunteer will never stop asking, but we need to be careful to guard our time. Deciding to simplify your life may be difficult to follow through on, but the rewards within your marriage and family will be worth it.

Since deciding to simplify my life, I have been asked to take on additional responsibility and I was able to say no several times now. It is a great feeling and I am learning how to better divide my time and talents.

I know that it would have been very easy for me to continue in these commitments and continue to juggle work, home, and outside obligations, but I am looking forward to slowing down and enjoying my time with Debby and the kids.

Health

Another challenge your relationship may be faced with is a major health crisis with you, your spouse, or your children. This can cause conflict within your marriage and challenges with the other children in your family as you cope with the debilitating illness or disease. It is not uncommon to see marriages crack under the strain of major medical difficulties within the immediate family.

There is nothing more precious to us than our family. Strip away all of our possessions and other relationships and leave us with only our family, and we would be content and blessed. I think most of you would agree that when your family is in danger, you would risk all that you have to protect them. When you cannot protect them from an injury or undefined illness, you may feel helpless and that is when you are most vulnerable to attack.

Unfortunately, we can speak from firsthand experience when it comes to family health challenges. We have been dealing with health concerns for over five years now, and for most of those five years we had no idea what the medical problems were. The fact that doctors cannot diagnose the medical conditions is both very concerning and frightening to us. I think I can say that not knowing is one of the worst parts of our ordeal.

Several years ago Debby had a long-term health mystery that was never really diagnosed. No matter what she did or what she ate, she was consistently losing weight and was down to nearly one hundred and ten pounds. We went to every type of specialist we could think of and she had nearly every type of test possible to diagnose the problem, but we never had resolution. In addition to the weight loss, she had a severe lung infection that took more than three months to heal.

I know what some of you must be thinking. An ability to eat fudge and chocolate cake and *still* lose weight? What's the problem? I've often joked that if I could package and sell whatever it was that was causing her weight loss, I'd be a very rich man!

Unfortunately, it was no laughing matter and she was sick for nearly two years. As suddenly as her weight loss started, it stopped. No explanation, no diagnosis, and more importantly for us, no closure. As you may imagine, those several years of doctor visits and the anticipation of a diagnosis were a major strain on Debby and the family.

Through it all, the most important thing I could do was to be there for her. I was able to adjust my work schedule as necessary for the multiple doctor appointments and tests, so I could be there with her if and when a doctor had some news. Looking back, I think that I was able to demonstrate a high level of concern to Debby by the way I was able to be there for her, and being there was more valuable to her than mere words could have expressed.

Just as Debby's health was improving, we were facing another health crisis. In May of 2007 we traveled to Pasco, Washington, for the state gymnastics competition that our youngest daughter was competing in. Pasco is a four-hour drive from where we live and it was pretty warm when we arrived there mid-afternoon.

Within the first half hour of being in our hotel, our second oldest daughter, Anna, collapsed and began to suffer a very intense migraine headache, coupled with other symptoms. She was lethargic, couldn't focus, and was on the verge of passing out. These symptoms came on very quickly. One moment she was laughing and bounding across the parking lot carrying her luggage, and then after getting up in the room and lying down on the couch, she began to crash rather quickly.

We took her to the local urgent care facility, but when we told them about her migraine headache and blurred vision, they turned us away and sent us to the emergency room at a hospital twenty minutes away in the next town over. They told us they were not qualified to handle a potential head injury. Leaving the rest of our family at the hotel with friends and grandparents, we took off for the hospital.

After hours of tests and evaluations at the hospital, including a spinal tap, she was diagnosed with simple dehydration and a migraine headache. We were given some medication and sent on our way. We left the hospital after midnight, and returned to the hotel with a very sick child. The following day after the competition, we came home and set a follow-up appointment with our pediatrician.

The next few months were filled with doctor visit after doctor visit, as her condition seemed to worsen. She was intolerant to heat and seemed to get very light-headed, to the point of fainting each time she exercised or did any physical activity. Climbing a set of stairs, something most of us take for granted, left her feeling exhausted and near collapse. Her symptoms include blurred vision, excessive fatigue, excessive thirst, dizziness, vertigo, and a slow heart rate.

For the next seven months we saw numerous doctors and specialists as we tried to find a diagnosis for her illness. It was a very frustrating and scary period for us all. We had both been accustomed to helping and caring for our children through whatever ailed them, until now. Anna's condition was continuing to worsen, with no answers available to us. I cannot begin to count all the visits to the pediatrician and the pediatric neurologist. It was a long, tiring, and trying time for the entire family.

After numerous doctor visits and tests, we finally found a specialist who gave us a diagnosis. It was definitely a defining moment. After nearly a year of the unknown, we knew what Anna was facing and could learn how to cope with the symptoms. We could move on to the next phase of our lives and we all could learn how to adjust to Anna's physical limitations.

By the time we got the diagnosis, Anna's health had deteriorated to the point where she could only attend school for two periods of the day and had to take classes on the Internet. For the rest of 2007, and continuing even today, she has had to modify what activities she can participate in.

Throughout the time that we were dealing with her medical condition with no diagnosis and no answer in sight, you can imagine the incredible stress we felt as parents. Knowing that our child was in pain and dealing with something we couldn't identify was terrifying to us. When there are no answers to a medical problem, people tend to think of the worst-case scenarios and struggle with the lack of medical intervention.

Through it all, we needed to maintain a positive attitude for our daughter, as she didn't know how to deal with these new limitations and challenges. It was very important that Debby and I communicated with each other and with her doctors concerning her condition. It would have been so easy to get frustrated and perhaps take our frustrations out on each other; but because of the closeness of our relationship, we have been able to weather the storms of doubt and the unknown.

It is all too common for a debilitating illness or life-altering event to cause families to drift apart. People deal with stress and the unknown in different ways, and this is another way in which marriages are tested. When parents begin to spend the majority of their time caring for a family member, the marriage relationship can suffer as a result. In addition, a natural response for some may be to find someone or something to blame for the illness, and an easy target for this blame could be the spouse. Rather than pulling together to navigate the current storm, one or both spouses may push the other away and isolate themselves in an effort to find answers and hope.

Another common reaction is to pull away from one another and turn all of one's attention on the sick child. After all, the spouse is healthy and strong and it's the child that needs all of the attention. It may be easy for a parent to justify this in his or her mind, but the consequences on the marriage are often disastrous. If you find yourself in a situation where a family member requires an unusual amount of time and attention, be careful not to care for them at the expense of meeting the needs of your spouse. You will need to be sure to continue to carve out time to cultivate your marriage and maintain a degree of normalcy in your relationship with your spouse.

During those times we made a diligent effort every day, no matter what the circumstances were, to be supportive and understanding of each other and of Anna. It is an ongoing effort even today, and we constantly rely on one another whenever we feel the circumstances are overwhelming. People often ask us how we cope with her illness and how we deal with the challenges. I always tell them that, thankfully for Anna, it is a life-altering illness, not a life-ending illness, so we have learned to modify her activities and live life the best way we can. Tomorrow's a new day and who knows what tomorrow will bring. Perhaps tomorrow will provide a medical breakthrough or a miraculous healing.

Through it all, remember that it is a conscious decision you make every day to love your spouse and to care for them in such a way that they know they are THE MOST IMPORTANT part of your life and that your marriage is the highest priority! With all the activities, pressures of life, sick children and ongoing demands that others put on us, we know we must rely on one another every day and choose to keep our relationship as the highest priority.

Job Loss

As I was picking up a newspaper recently, the headlines were screaming out things like, "Additional Lay-offs to be Announced" and "Plant Closure Shocks Close-knit Community." In nearly every economic climate there is the potential for work slowdowns and lay-offs, but in the current economic climate we are living in it seems to be the rule rather than the exception. Living in Seattle, where there are numerous companies that are at the pinnacle of their market sector announcing job cuts that number in the thousands, it's pretty easy to get depressed when thinking about job security. Between the airplane, coffee, and computer industry leaders, there are tens of thousands of lay-off notices that have been announced and are currently being handed out. There are many people I know who have either lost their job due to the economic slowdown or are in fear of losing their job. Either way, it can have devastating effects on individuals and families.

I can't imagine what it feels like to walk out of your boss's office after just being told that you no longer have a job, but I have seen firsthand how various people react to that news. For some, they have the confidence that their skills will enable them to find another job that can replace their lost income. For others, they fall into a serious depression and have no idea where their next paycheck will come from. I know people who have been out of work for months on end and have absolutely no prospects of finding gainful employment.

Having your economic security blanket pulled out from under you is a very unsettling experience. There may be questions that arise for which you don't have the answers, and there are numerous feelings you may endure. Feelings of helplessness, anger, frustration, or even incompetence are common emotions you may experience. You may not have money set aside for emergencies and this is bound to raise the level of helplessness you may feel.

In addition to losing a paycheck, there are other aspects of your life that may be impacted when you lose a job. You may lose health benefits, retirement benefits, 401k matching funds, etc. You may have paid a deposit on a family vacation destination but without a job you may not be able to take the vacation time you had planned, causing you to forfeit the deposit. A job loss has the potential to impact your family in ways you may not even comprehend until you face the reality yourself.

We have covered financial stress in an earlier chapter, but we were primarily addressing financial planning and budgeting. We were working with the assumption that you are gainfully employed and have an income that you can base your family budget on. What do you do then, when you don't have that income and you struggle to find a good paying job?

A job loss often impacts the family with considerable and devastating results that can go far beyond the bottom line of a balance sheet on your computer financial software program. I believe that even in the worst economic conditions, there is work available. While you may not be able to secure the job that is ideal for your family needs, I encourage you to make it your full-time job to get out and find a job. Once you find a job—and don't be too picky if you have no income at the moment—then you can find a better job. Rather than turn down a job because the compensation package isn't comparable to the job you lost, take the job; start the flow of income again, and then focus your efforts on securing a better job. You may need to do this several times, but that's oaky. It probably took you several years to get to the level of compensation that you were at previously, so don't have lofty expectations that you will only accept a job with an identical compensation package to that which you lost.

> A single friend, one of the opposite sex, is always a potential threat to your marriage.

Outside Influences

Often in a marriage there are outside influences that affect the health of the marriage. In fact, in every marriage there are outside influences that have the potential of affecting the marriage, both in positive and negative ways. Oftentimes you or your spouse may begin to build a friendship with someone who could potentially threaten the marriage. Anyone who doesn't support marriage, in general, is a threat. Anyone who has different ideas, values, or morals could potentially influence a spouse in such a way that begins to break down the marriage bond. We must all be extremely careful when building and maintaining friendships with others. It is vital that they support you and your spouse and that any advise or influence they have be positive and supportive of your marriage.

One negative idea or statement is all it may take to begin to plant ideas in your head and create feelings of animosity toward your spouse. Even someone who is in a different stage in their life may give advice contrary to the investment you are making in your marriage. A single friend, one of the opposite sex, is always a potential threat to your marriage. Likewise, a friend who is in a struggling marriage themselves or who feels that they have settled for something less than they wanted in

135

their own marriage, could be a potential threat. These types of friends, and many other examples, may make comments to you or give you advice that is unhealthy for your marriage. They may actually cause you to think negative thoughts about your marriage or question your marriage commitment.

You must always have your guard up and be on the lookout for those who do not give good, positive advice when it comes to your marriage. If you find that the influence from your friends is not supportive of your relationship with your spouse, you may need to consider distancing yourself from those friends to avoid following their negative influence or advice.

Jealousy

When you and I think of jealousy in the realm of marriage, the first thing that most likely comes to mind is jealousy of another man or woman. While this is a real and significant threat, there is another aspect of jealousy that we see in the world that could be just as devastating to a relationship. This aspect of jealousy can build up over time and increase in intensity without you even knowing it. This is jealousy you may have of one another.

In most relationships, one person most likely has a job that can be viewed as more "significant" than the other. One of you may be in a job that carries more prestige in the community, or one of you may be more popular and well-known in your community. One of you may make significantly more money than the other or one of you may choose to stay at home with the children and not work outside of the home at all. These are just a few reasons that could lead to jealousy within a relationship. All of these examples, when not held in check, have the potential to create a negative impact on the attitude of one or both spouses and could lead to resentment, anger, and even contempt.

It is dangerous for one of you to think that you are better than your spouse, and it is devastating to the relationship if you verbally talk down to your spouse or make him or her feel that they are insignificant. You can do this unknowingly, through little comments that may seem insignificant to you. An attitude of self-righteousness has the potential to set unrealistic expectations or goals that your spouse thinks he or she needs to live up to. Imagine living in someone's shadow, never feeling as if your opinions count and never thinking that you are an equal partner in your relationship.

It must be recognized and accepted that the role that each of you are playing in your relationship are of equal importance and that you are both contributing to the relationship. Neither can be thought of as more important or above the other. Each spouse must learn to value the other and recognize the value that the other contributes to the marriage. Each of you must also believe that you are significant and contributing to your marriage, and accept and value the role that you play. You both bring unique qualities to the relationship and it is important that you continually build one another up, without allowing feelings of inferiority to creep in.

Jacob, for example, has a position on the city council and is recognized throughout the community. His wife Caroline needs to be careful not to allow herself to feel that he is more significant than she is, simply because of the high profile nature of his occupation. Just because his chosen profession or career puts him in the public spotlight, that has no impact on the contribution they each make to their relationship. If she allows feelings of inferiority to creep into her mind, she may begin to resent her husband and secretly crave the attention he gets. She may begin to feel jealous of the attention others give to Jacob and desire that level of attention herself. On the other hand, Jacob also needs to be careful not to bask in the attention of the spotlight and leave Caroline out in the dark. He must continually be aware of her feelings and include her in every aspect of his life that he can.

Throughout the majority of our married life, Debby has been a stay-at-home mom. We have always valued the time she has been able to spend with our children and we have never regretted that decision. However, she has experienced some of these feelings firsthand in our own marriage. She has felt the pains of resentment and anger, feeling at times that she was stuck at home while I was able to go off to work every day and therefore enjoy a break from the routines of the household. There are too many families that do not have the privilege of a stay-at-home mom or dad, and we know that the investment we are making in our children will have significant returns later in their lives.

In our own relationship, we work through these very issues from time to time. It is important that I continually encourage and remind Debby of how important her work with our children really is. I encourage Debby

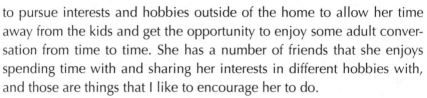
to pursue interests and hobbies outside of the home to allow her time away from the kids and get the opportunity to enjoy some adult conversation from time to time. She has a number of friends that she enjoys spending time with and sharing her interests in different hobbies with, and those are things that I like to encourage her to do.

Over the past couple of years, primarily while we were dealing with Anna's sickness, she met with many of her girlfriends for coffee at least two or three times a week. Whether she is helping a friend through the challenges of her marriage, talking about Anna's progress, or just catching up with an old friend, she values her coffee meetings and they are now an important part of her routine.

Biblical Perspective

We don't always understand why something turned out wrong or why things happened as they did, but we trust God and know that He holds all things in His hands. It is reassuring to remember that nothing surprises God. He didn't look down from his throne and say "Oops, I missed that one." It may be easy for people to think that God is so busy with the other six billion plus people in this world

> He often allows us to go through the trials and tribulations to prepare us for what's to come. He tests us to purify our hearts.

that He momentarily lost track of what we are doing, but we know that is not the case. I think of this song we teach our young kids and remember that it is the truth—He does know what is going on in each of our lives and there is a reason for it: "He's got the whole world, in His hands, He's got the whole world, in His hands. . . ."

You see, He not only knows exactly what is happening in our lives, He knows how He is going to use our circumstances for His glory. We don't always understand or see through the pain we are currently suffering, but He assures us that "we are His workmanship, created in Christ Jesus, for every good work." (Eph. 2:10) He often allows us to go through the trials and tribulations to prepare us for what's to come. He tests us to purify our hearts.

Pastor Tom Schrader says that, "God intended difficulty and hardships in our lives because He loves us." It's for our good and His glory, and sometimes we need these difficult times to teach us how to live. These hard times teach us how to respond to trials in the future. God may be using a trial or hardship to prepare you for a future trial that He knows will be much bigger and will require you to be stronger in your faith. Today's mountain you're facing may be the proving grounds for your faithfulness and endurance, which He will use to encourage someone else in the future. Romans 8:28 says, "And we know that God causes everything to work together for the good of those who love God and are called according to His purpose for them."

Think about this: God may be preparing you to intercede in the life of someone in your circle of influence at some point in your future. The end results of these trials we go through are not always for us; sometimes they are simply used to point to Him during the trial or they may be for someone else entirely. Rather than exert time and energy trying to understand why God is allowing something to happen, we should instead focus on what we can learn from it and grow from the experience. My primary prayer for Anna over these last couple years has been for complete healing. However, I've also prayed diligently that Debby and I are faithful and that we continue to trust God throughout this illness. When it's all over with and she is healed, I want to be able to look back and know that we were faithful, as Job was in the Old Testament, and that we passed the test.

Oftentimes we all put additional stress on ourselves as we analyze situations that we deal with. Rather than working through a problem, you may find yourself breaking down each detail to see where you could have made a different choice or somehow avoided the situation completely.

In the movie "The Curious Case of Benjamin Button" there is a scene where they do just that. A dancer gets hit by a car, and the scene takes the viewers through the moments before the car accident, analyzing the activities and events that led up to the accident as if to determine what different choices she could have made for the outcome to be different. If only her alarm clock woke her up on time, or if she didn't break her heel while she was running to catch the taxi. If only . . .

In many cases, such as Anna's illness, there may be nothing you could have done to avoid the current crisis you are in, so why invest so much emotional capital on trying to isolate the cause? People have a tendency to run so many "if onlys" through their minds that they miss the lesson that lies within the trial. It may be that you will never know the answer to these questions, this side of Glory.

God's Word tells us in Ephesians 6:10–17 to put on the whole armor of God. This is not something we are to do only once, when we accept Christ as our Savior. No, this is to be a daily ritual, a daily exercise of your faith. When we put on this armor, we are prepared to face the daily challenges that life throws our way and then we are better prepared to withstand the fiery darts of the devil.

Verse 13 in this same passage says that after we have put on His armor, we can stand firm. The NIV translation says, "and after you have done everything, to stand." That gives me encouragement, knowing that I can be prepared to stand fast against anything that life throws my way. I can face sickness, job loss, financial ruin, and pressure from any angle, knowing that God will see me through. Philippians 1:6 says, "And I am certain that God, who began the good work within you, will continue his work until it is finally finished on the day when Christ Jesus returns." With this promise, we are assured that we can face the various attacks against our marriage and in the end, we will stand firm.

As I read through this chapter again and thought about each of the ways marriages are under attack, one thought continued to come to mind: disappointment. Disappointment is a common emotion we feel in each of these attacks. When we let disappointment rule and take hold of our heart and life, we begin to see things through a different lens, with a different perspective. If you are continually disappointed in someone or in your circumstances, the tendency seems to be to lower your expectations and actually begin to expect to be disappointed. How tragic.

God provides us hope for a better tomorrow and the promise that He will provide for your every need, no matter how large or small. When I am reminded that not a single sparrow falls from the sky without His knowledge (Matthew 10:29), I am encouraged that He knows about my problems and my disappointments, and I can turn to Him for answers.

He can turn your sorrows into joy (Jeremiah 31:13); your mourning into dancing (Psalm 30:11); your suffering into healing (Mark 5:34); and your hope will not lead to disappointment (Romans 5:5). He is your all in all (Ephesians 1:23 KJV), the joy of your salvation (Psalm 51:12). And Romans 8:17 tells us that our inheritance is in Him.

Chapter 10

Protect Your Amazing Marriage Against Infidelity

"To stand firm in the battle for our marriages, we must be prepared. We can never assume that having a good marriage shelters us from temptation. In this age of "anything goes," the wise woman will purposefully build walls around her marriage ahead of time to help close the door on opportunities for temptation."

~ Judy Starr

There are many ways marriages need to be protected. We could all get distracted with our time, with our emotions, with our hobbies and interests, and even with our careers. Perhaps the biggest danger to a relationship is a slow fade. When we slowly slip away from each other and increase the time spent apart, our interests may begin to include activities or people other than our spouse. If you find yourselves spending more time apart than time together, you are inviting trouble. We encourage you to do things apart, and to have separate hobbies and activities, but when the majority of your time is spent away from one another, you may begin to feel comfortable being apart and it becomes easier and easier to do things separately.

When this happens, your interest in your spouse and marriage may slowly fade away as you drift apart, and this usually happens without you realizing how it is affecting your relationship. You may wake up one morning alone, while your spouse is off pursuing a lower golf score or the elusive fish that always seems to always get away, and you may wonder what happened to the breakfasts you once shared. The rounds of golf, the fishing trips, the scrapbook overnighters, the shopping sprees with your girlfriends, and the like seem rare and innocent when they first begin, but over time they increase in both number and importance, and before you know it, the two of you rarely spend time together doing the things you once cherished.

When you spend increasing amounts of time away from one another, you may begin to look elsewhere for encouragement, emotional support, and acceptance. If you are not spending the quality time with your spouse that you once did, you still have basic human needs that must be fulfilled and you may try to find it somewhere else. In very few cases is it just the sexual needs that get fulfilled outside of your marriage; it usually begins with the emotional needs.

Your emotional needs may no longer be satisfied by your spouse, and these needs must be met. If you spend time away from your spouse and your activities involve people of the opposite gender, the chance is greater that you may develop a friendship with someone which could develop into something deeper. This friend may be the one who gives you the encouragement and emotional support you need but that your spouse no longer fulfills. Once the emotional needs are met, the die is cast for this relationship to move beyond emotions and into the physical realm.

Most of us, male and female alike, may think nothing of having a best friend or a good friend of the opposite gender, other than their spouse. We believe that confiding in anyone of the opposite sex, outside of your marriage, could be detrimental to your relationship and could potentially lead to disaster in your marriage. The risk is too high that you could easily begin to confide personal and intimate details to the other person and begin to slowly build feelings for them. It is too easy to find comfort away from your spouse, especially when there are issues within the marriage and one or both spouses are seeking support and encouragement elsewhere.

Allowing someone of the opposite gender to influence your marriage disguised as a friend carries many risks. The risk of becoming increasingly attached to the friend and less bonded with your spouse is just begging for division in your marriage. We are not suggesting that you cannot or should not have any friends of the opposite gender, but we suggest that contact must be kept in check and there must be guidelines in place for this friendship. Your closest friends and confidants should not be opposite gender friends. Additionally, your spouse should always be included in the process of drawing up these guidelines. The guidelines should be followed closely and either spouse should be allowed veto power with no questions asked.

In your everyday dealings, there are many things we believe to be inappropriate and may put you at risk in compromising your marriage.

There are some simple steps that will protect you and help you avoid compromising circumstances, or something that may appear to others to be inappropriate. One thing you should avoid is one-on-one encounters or meetings with someone of the opposite gender, such as business or social meals. If circumstances beyond your control dictate that you must meet alone with someone of the opposite gender other than your spouse, meet in as public and conspicuous a place as possible, and let your spouse know exactly where you will be and how long your meeting should last. We recommend that you never ride in a car with someone of the opposite gender who is not a family member. This is simply for accountability and avoiding any appearance of wrongdoing.

Women tend to be more emotionally dependent than men, and women need to guard their hearts more closely when it comes to who they confide in and ultimately who they entrust their heart to. Only your spouse deserves your whole heart.

Men are typically much more visually stimulated than women and we men need to continually stay on guard and wary of our minds and the information we feed into our heads. We must be on constant alert and be discerning of what we read, what we watch, and the conversations we have. Debby wants to share a few things on this topic.

Jason travels overnight five to six times a year. He has what we call a "safety net" in place. He calls his friend Mark to let him know he will be traveling and when he will be gone. After Jason returns home, he calls Mark again and they talk about how the trip went. Mark asks him the tough questions that they set up ahead of time. Questions such as: "Did you order or watch pornography or any other inappropriate television in your hotel room?" or "Was there anyone in particular you were attracted to or that caught your eye?" Other questions may be, "Did you go anywhere or do anything in which you would be ashamed or embarrassed to tell your wife?"

This could be a very brief discussion or a long conversation, depending on the circumstances of the trip. As Jason's wife, I appreciate this process very much because I know that Mark has our best interest at heart and I know he will be bold and ask Jason the tough questions.

Developing a relationship with someone of the same gender that will ask you the tough questions very well may keep you from making poor choices. I love the accountability they have to each other, and I know Jason is much less likely to do anything to put our marriage or himself at risk because of the questions he knows he will need to answer when he returns. Jason, in turn, does the same thing for Mark and his wife when Mark travels. The accountability goes both ways and is mutually supportive. I'll let Jason take it from here.

One thing that Debby and I often joke about is the phrase, "I'm married but I'm not dead." Or, "It doesn't matter where you get your appetite as long as you come home for dinner." This is just reality. We think it is extremely important for you to realize and acknowledge that you will, at some point in your marriage, be attracted to someone other than your spouse, if only for a fleeting moment. Understanding this and being prepared for it is an important component to protecting your marriage.

The key to dealing with this attraction successfully depends entirely on how you respond to this attraction. Will you hide it from your spouse, or will you be honest and discuss your feelings so you can have a united front in your marriage as you guard against infidelity?

Allowing feelings for someone other than your spouse, no matter how remote they may be, to foster unchecked is a recipe for disaster. It is not only dangerous, but it is also dishonest. One of the worst things you can do is to pretend that it doesn't exist, because in reality it does exist and the feeling may become stronger as time goes by if you don't address your feelings.

Physical attractions aren't always something you can control, and being attracted to someone isn't wrong. Seeing a drop-dead gorgeous woman or a stunningly handsome man and being attracted to that person isn't something we can control. What you can and must control is your thought process and how you deal with that attraction. Looking at a beautiful woman is not wrong. Looking at a beautiful woman with lust in your heart and pursuing those thoughts . . . now that, my friend, is inappropriate.

Two other very serious issues that have the potential to divide spouses and cause problems in marriage are the Internet and cell phones. With the Internet, the sky is the limit with regards to potentially meeting, communicating, and going too far with someone other than your spouse. It used to be that the risks were only within an immediate realm of influence such as the workplace, the gym, the grocery store, or even your church, parish, or synagogue. Now all a person has to do is sign onto the Internet, do a quick search, and, voila, an affair is waiting to happen, delivered right into your own home.

While it may seem absurd to you, and it does to me, there are Internet sites with the sole purpose of destroying your marriage. Besides the obvious threats from pornographic websites, there are actual websites that promote extra-marital affairs and that teach you step-by-step how to have an affair discreetly. They outline how to meet someone and provide a method of communicating with others for the sole purpose of engaging in an affair. They provide tips on covering your tracks and keeping your secrets from your spouse and friends. I ask myself, is nothing sacred anymore?

> Guarding against intruders is vital to building, achieving, and maintaining an amazing marriage.

Guarding against intruders is vital to building, achieving, and maintaining an amazing marriage. We cannot say enough about accountability when it comes to the preservation and protection of your marriage against intruders. We all have our strengths and weaknesses, and given the right set of circumstances you may find yourself facing a situation that you aren't prepared for. Having an accountability partner may very well increase your awareness of the risks and empower you to maintain your credibility.

With regard to the Internet, Debby and I give each other full access to any and all screen names and computers we may be using at any given time. We know each other's passwords and we have an understanding that if the passwords change, we must inform each other of the change and why. This is not a privacy issue; it is a matter of respect. We respect each other enough to let the other have access to every corner of our lives. It is not a lack of trust, rather a measure of confidence in one another and a willingness to be completely open and transparent. There is no area that is off limits in our marriage. If one of us asks for access to anything it is granted, and a discussion follows with regard to the reasons why, if necessary.

Spouses owe it to each other to be honest and transparent with regards to concerns the other may have and they should always be brought up in a discussion. Not only does transparency and honesty help guard your heart, but it protects your marriage as well.

We cannot stress enough how important it is to have accountability when it comes to the Internet. The Internet is a potentially devastating threat to your marriage that must be reined in. Gaining access to pornography through the Internet is becoming more and more prevalent, and if you think your marriage is protected without safeguards in place, you may be fooling yourself. Spouses should have access at all times to one another's computers, and computers that are used between home and work (laptops) should be no exception. Shared access to every password and every computer is important and sends a message to your spouse that you encourage and invite accountability.

The other issue that we feel is very serious and needs to be addressed is the use of the cell phone. Home phones are being utilized less often than in the past and cell phones are usually in the hands of everyone in the household; not just in the hands of the parents but the children as well. This makes each spouse readily available, usually twenty-four hours a day, to anyone and everyone who has been given access to that number.

The primary means of contact for someone intruding in a marriage is usually the cell phone. Cell phone call histories and text messages are easily erased and the choice to silence or mute the phone makes access without detection far too easy. Full access should be granted to your spouse at all times without question. Now, I have never asked Debby for her cell phone so I could check the history, but I know that if I were to ask, she would grant me access without hesitation.

Just as with the Internet, allowing access to one another's cell phones without question builds value and trust in your marriage. The moment a spouse denies access, a seed of doubt is planted; and if left to grow and take root, it could potentially destroy the marriage. Transparency and accountability are vital components of your marriage.

Biblical Perspective

Finding a biblical perspective on protecting your marriage from infidelity isn't difficult. What is difficult, is deciding which angle to discuss and which verses to include. God created marriage to be a binding covenant between a man and a woman and He desires that the marriage bed be undefiled and that we remain faithful to one another. Hebrews 13:4 says, "Give honor to marriage, and remain faithful to one another in marriage. God will surely judge people who are immoral and those who commit adultery." Knowing how God views the covenant of marriage, how can we take steps to protect ourselves and keep our marriage pure?

An answer to that question can be found in 1 Thessalonians 4:3–8, where it says, "God's will is for you to be holy, so stay away from all sexual sin. Then each of you will control his own body and live in holiness and honor—not in lustful passion like the pagans who do not know God and his ways. Never harm or cheat a Christian brother in this matter by violating his wife, for the Lord avenges all such sins, as we have solemnly warned you before. God has called us to live holy lives, not impure lives. Therefore, anyone who refuses to live by these rules is not disobeying human teaching but is rejecting God, who gives his Holy Spirit to you." Keeping your marriage pure involves making proper choices to remain faithful to one another as well as taking action to protect against intruders preying on your spouse.

> Keeping your marriage pure involves making proper choices

As we discussed in this chapter, maintaining proper relationships with others is a critical aspect of guarding your heart and protecting your marriage. Proverbs 4:23 says, "Guard your heart above all else, for it determines the course of your life." 1 John 1:8 says, "If we claim we have no sin, we are only fooling ourselves and not living in the truth." Just because you proclaim Christ and He lives within you, that alone does not keep you from sin. You are fooling yourselves if you think that you are immune to the temptations around you simply because you are Christian. Although the Bible does tell us that there is always a way of escaping all temptations, you must realize we are all born with a sinful nature and we all succumb to temptation and sin from time to time. Guarding your heart and putting up a protective wall around your marriage is essential.

Guarding your heart includes being careful what you fill your mind with. I think of the cliché used with computers that says, "Garbage in, garbage out." If you don't properly program the computer, it can't perform the way you want it to. If you put garbage into your mind and fill your minds eye with lustful desires, they will come out at some point. Matthew 5:28 says, "But I say, anyone who even looks at a woman with lust has already committed adultery with her in his heart." The fateful adulterous relationship that David had with Bathsheba in 2 Samuel chapter 2 began with David watching her bathe on the rooftop. The text says that he was walking on the palace rooftop and saw a woman of unusual beauty taking a bath. If he had noticed this and turned away to give her privacy, he could have avoided the sin of adultery and murder. However, his eyes lingered and he began to desire what he saw. When you fill your mind with fantasies and desires, you are apt to begin to formulate in your heart how to get what you want. To avoid this trap, think on things of God (Philippians 4:8).

One topic that many people avoid talking about is the issue of "whose body is it, anyhow?" In a covenant marriage, we give of ourselves to our spouse and we no longer have control over our own bodies. This is addressed in 1 Corinthians 7:1–6 in this manner, "Now regarding the questions you asked in your letter. Yes, it is good to live a celibate life. But because there is so much sexual immorality, each man should have his own wife, and each woman should have her own husband. The husband should fulfill his wife's sexual needs, and the wife should fulfill her husband's needs. The wife gives authority over her body to her husband, and the husband gives authority over his body to his wife. Do not deprive each other of sexual relations, unless you both agree to refrain from sexual intimacy for a limited time so you can give yourselves more completely to prayer. Afterward, you should come together again so that Satan won't be able to tempt you because of your lack of self-control. I say this as a concession, not as a command." What is clear here is that you are not to deprive your spouse of sex, which could open the door to temptation and poor choices.

Temptation leads to desire, which leads to sin, which leads to death, according to James 1:14–15, ". . . each one is tempted when, by his own evil desire, he is dragged away and enticed. Then, after desire has conceived, it gives birth to sin; and sin, when it is full-grown, gives birth to death" (NIV) and that is a dangerous recipe for infidelity. Avoid areas, acquaintances, and activities you know will lead to temptation. Establish boundaries in your relationship, develop an accountability partner, and guard your heart. By doing these things, you will be protecting your marriage.

We'll let 1 Corinthians 10:13 have the last word, "No temptation has seized you except what is common to man. And God is faithful; he will not let you be tempted beyond what you can bear. But when you are tempted, he will also provide a way out so that you can stand up under it." (NIV)

Chapter 11

Key Elements of an Amazing Marriage

"Sometimes the most basic elements are the most fascinating, the most absorbing, and also the most complicated." ~ Virginia Graham

In the preceding chapters, we addressed a number of topics that we consider to be basic fundamentals of an amazing marriage. This chapter recaps of some of the most critical elements of an amazing marriage and explores several of these in more depth. Anyone who truly loves another and is willing to put in the necessary time and commitment can achieve an amazing marriage. The topics we discuss in the following pages aren't the sum total of what is required, but we believe they compose the foundational truths necessary for success and excellence.

Trust

"Reliance on the integrity, strength, ability, surety, etc., of a person or thing; confidence. The obligation or responsibility imposed on a person in whom confidence or authority is placed"[1]

Trust is one of the primary foundations of a healthy relationship. There's not much you can build in your relationship if there is an absence of trust. Trust, after all, is the cornerstone of marriage. We trust that our spouse has pledged complete and unending love and commitment to us. We trust that our spouse has our best interests at heart. We trust that our spouse fully intends to spend the rest of his or her life with us, regardless of the circumstances that may change. We trust that our spouse will love us unconditionally, and that if all we own is stripped away, our spouse will still be there loving and caring for us. Finally, we trust that there is nothing in the world more important to our spouse than us and our relationship.

---

1 http://dictionary.reference.com/browse/trust

So what is trust anyway? Blind faith? Not hardly. As *Webster* defines it, there are numerous meanings of the word trust, in both the noun and verb form. Some of the more applicable definitions in the noun form include "the trait of trusting; of believing in the honesty and reliability of others." Trust is also defined as "complete confidence in a person or plan." As a verb, trust is defined as "having confidence or faith in; allowing without fear."[2]

As we relate trust to relationships, it is easy to see that if there is not a complete trust in one's spouse, the marriage relationship cannot thrive, much less survive. Trust is an integral part of our relationship as a married couple and it is the glue that holds us together. Having complete confidence in a person to love us, no matter our faults or circumstances, is truly a rare and unique experience.

Trust means having a complete assurance that circumstances will not influence the relationship we share with one another. The vow that many of us have taken that states "for better or for worse, in sickness and in health" simplifies this concept of trust. If we entered into a relationship that was based on circumstances, it would be so easy for the marriage to dissolve at the first sign of trouble. Trust, therefore, means complete confidence in one another, which is vital to the healthy growth of a marriage relationship. Without trust, a relationship is destined for failure and disappointment.

Integrity

"Adherence to moral and ethical principles; soundness of moral character; honesty."[3]

Integrity, just like trust, is foundational and essential in the marriage relationship. Integrity encompasses trust, but is more clearly defined as moral soundness. I've heard it said that integrity means doing the right thing, even when no one is watching. I add that integrity is doing the right thing *because* it is the right thing, not because someone else expects you to do it. In the marriage relationship, integrity means remaining true to your spouse and avoiding situations that are potentially destructive to your

---

2 http://www.websters-online-dictionary.org/definition/trust
3 http://dictionary.reference.com/browse/integrity

relationship. Integrity can also mean avoiding situations that evade or avoid responsible actions.

The majority of us would like to think that we have integrity and we would also like to think that others see us as having high moral character. We all desire and expect this behavior in our spouse. It is one of the foundational truths of any successful marriage that both marriage partners posses and exercise personal responsibility and integrity.

When I exhibit integrity as a virtue and a character trait, it builds respect from Debby. When she sees me holding myself to a higher standard and following a sound moral compass, the level of respect she has for me increases. However, being as though I am not perfect and make poor choices from time to time, when I fail to uphold those expectations and do or say something unexpected and regrettable, she can look at the overall track record of my integrity and realize that whatever the offense was, it was an aberration and not consistent with my habits. There are times when we both say and do regrettable things or make poor choices, but they don't shake our commitment to one another or destroy our marriage.

Integrity certainly does not mean perfection; rather, it is a character trait that one strives to achieve through a combination of decisions and actions. A person known to be of high integrity is not one who never makes mistakes or never has a lapse in judgment, but someone who generally makes wise decisions and who puts a high premium on making good choices. It is one who takes responsibility for his or her own actions and is consistent, regardless of circumstances.

Integrity can be defined as the strength of one's will to stand for something or to hold something in high regard. In our marriage covenant, it is the covenant of marriage itself and the sanctity of marriage that is held in high regard and protected from dangers that can come from any and all directions. Integrity in marriage refers not only to complete honesty, but also to the moral obligation you have toward your spouse to remain faithful and true in all things, but especially in terms of your sexual relationship.

There are truly few things that can destroy a marriage quicker than a spouse who lacks integrity in the sexual realm. Infidelity immediately destroys the foundational trust in a marriage and could potentially take years to rebuild. Integrity can be restored provided both partners renew their commitment to one another and their commitment to make the marriage work, at all cost.

Unconditional Love

"Affection or commitment with no limits or conditions; not subject to a condition or conditions; absolute and complete love"[4]

As you will see, the majority of the topics in this chapter are closely intertwined and related to one another. Unconditional love is one of those fundamental truths that must be present for any relationship to grow and prosper. If your love for one another is conditional, it cannot and will not be eternal. Conditional love is dependent upon a specific set of circumstances or criteria. It changes and adjusts when the circumstances change. Unconditional love means that regardless of the circumstances and storms you may face in life, your love will stay the course and remain faithful and true.

We believe that love is a conscious decision to care for your spouse in such a way as to meet their needs and exceed their expectations every day. It is a selfless love that puts the other first, in all things, and that demonstrates your commitment.

It is important to establish unconditional love early in your relationship, even when the challenges seem small and insignificant. Time doesn't necessarily work the same in all relationships and most of us aren't on a textbook-style timeframe. By that, I mean that your love won't necessarily be tested with a progression of challenges, starting with something small and insignificant in the beginning and growing with intensity over time. Some relationships are thrust into challenging waters at the very onset of the relationship, as ours was, while others may have the luxury of developing a long-term relationship before facing adversity.

As you love your spouse unconditionally and prove your love time and time again, their self-esteem and confidence in the relationship grows. Their value rises and they in turn are drawn into a deeper love for you. One popular marriage author describes the relationship between a man and a woman as a bank account. The more positive things you say and do, the more deposits you make in your account. On the other hand, every time you make a thoughtless comment or commit a foolish and selfish act, your account is debited. The idea then is to have a positive balance, just like in your checkbook, and to make more deposits than debits to maintain peace and harmony in your relationship.

---

4 http://dictionary.reference.com/browse/unconditional+love

There is nothing more beautiful than two people who truly love one another with an unconditional love. There are no motives, no schemes, no enticements, and no manipulations. Unconditional love doesn't require deposits, it doesn't require favors, and it doesn't require bribes. Unconditional love is one person loving another, regardless of circumstances, and regardless of any reciprocal act or behavior. They love because that is what they do, that is the choice they make, and nothing can change that fact. Unconditional love is a choice; one that chooses to stand the test of time and the test of circumstances.

Resolve

"Firmness of purpose or intent; determination."[5]

Resolve may not be one of the words you would have chosen if you were putting together a list of absolute requirements, but as it relates to marriage and unconditional love, we believe it is one of the essential elements of a successful and amazing marriage. Resolve, or tenacity, and determination will get you through when the storms of life are pounding away

> Unconditional love is one person loving another, regardless of circumstances

at your anchor. They will allow you to stand firm, without wavering in your convictions. Without having a predetermined resolve that you will stick by your spouse when life gets tough, thoughts of doubt and despair may creep in and begin to take hold in your heart.

It is no secret or surprise that bad things happen in life. Sickness, job loss, disappointment, financial setbacks, and countless other challenges appear in our path on a continual basis. Challenges and problems cannot be avoided and oftentimes cannot be controlled, much less result in a chosen outcome. What you can control, however, when you face these trials and tribulations is your response to them. How will you handle these setbacks? Who will you turn to for comfort, and who will you turn to for solutions? Will you play the blame game and try to find fault in others, or will you accept the fact that bad things do happen to good people and work together to find a way out of the mess you are in? The answer lies in your resolve and commitment to one another.

---

5 http://dictionary.reference.com/browse/resolve

People respond to crisis in different ways, and some people immediately look to find fault in others. Their financial troubles certainly can't be a result of their own choices. It must have been caused by someone else. Someone else gave a poor investment recommendation; otherwise your 401k would not be reflecting the loss that it is. The termination notice your boss handed you is obviously part of a bigger financial crisis your company is facing and cannot at all be associated with your work ethic and the choices you've made.

Can you see how easy it is to fall prey and victim to your circumstances and how easy it is to find fault in your spouse for your current or ongoing problems? Resolve and total commitment to one another is paramount in determining the success in your relationship. It is a mindset that no matter what happens in your relationship you must maintain the tenacity to stay the course. Even if your spouse gives up and doesn't seem to care anymore, you must determine in your heart to stay the course, no matter how long it takes, and trust that he or she will respond. Resolve to love your spouse, regardless of the circumstances that come your way and learn from every setback and failure.

Compromise

"A settlement of differences by mutual concessions"[6]

In an amazing marriage, compromise is a concept that we feel is crucial to success. Compromise, as we define it, simply means that individually you must give up so together you can go up. There will be times when you need to sacrifice what you want as an individual in order to get what you need as a couple, or to get what your spouse needs. Oftentimes we have wants, perceived needs, and desires that we try to pursue, but perhaps at the expense of our relationship. There are times when we need to set aside our individual desires for the sake of the relationship and make compromises.

A large part of compromise begins with acceptance. Accept your spouse for what and who he or she is. This is an aspect of the unconditional love we discussed earlier. Your spouse is a unique individual with different skills and abilities, as well as a unique personality and unique

6 http://dictionary.reference.com/browse/compromise

character traits. Accept them for who and what they are. You really can't change a person to a large degree, and it is important to value your spouse and accept them as they are. There are some obvious reasons your spouse was attractive to you initially, but undoubtedly there are some things that you wish you could change about your spouse. However, you may not be in a position to change them as much as you'd like to.

We hear a lot about acceptance in our society. We are told that we are to blindly accept differences in one another and work toward the goal of unity. That sounds good, but what if he is a habitual drug user? What if she has anger management issues and continually threatens your children? I think we could all agree that those are qualities that we would not want to accept. Too often a concept or a principle that sounds good cannot be applied across all situations, all circumstances, and all people.

Rather than blindly accept who your mate is, we suggest that you understand where the point of acceptance is. There are obviously some habits you would not and should not change. These need to be recognized and understood. There could be many things that your spouse does that may seem trivial or even a slight annoyance to you, but they are a part of who he or she is. There may be something that they value that you don't see as having any worth whatsoever, but you need to allow them the freedom of individualism. There are also some things that you just don't consider important enough to influence for a change.

However, some traits or behaviors may prove to be damaging to your relationship, and you must face and address those. Oftentimes these are not identified or realized prior to marriage and they may come as a surprise to you. What are you to do if you find yourself in a marriage commitment and then discover less-than-desirable behaviors from your spouse? You are not expected to be a doormat, yet there's not much that you can really change in someone else if they don't want to change. So, how do you cope with potentially harmful habits or behaviors?

The first step is to identify the behavior. Identify and clarify what it is that you feel is either harmful or potentially harmful, and identify it in as clear a manner as possible. Avoid generalities, and be as specific as possible.

The next step is to discuss the behavior with your spouse. As you do this, be conscientious of how your spouse may feel upon hearing this from you. Explain your feelings clearly and specifically, but not in an offensive and condemning tone. Don't criticize or condemn your spouse, but make it clear that you disapprove of or are fearful of the particular behavior. Include your potential fears and why it is that you feel the way you do. It is important to note that if you feel danger in any way, either have this discussion in a public setting or take a close friend with you who can be both supportive and protective at the same time.

Let your spouse know that you love him or her, unconditionally, yet be very specific in what your concerns are. In many cases, when you approach someone with a spirit of love and concern, he or she will be more open to consider your feelings than if you attack in a manner that undermines and belittles them. Above all else, be loving and respectful, while being honest with your feelings.

If you address a concern with your spouse in a loving and nonconfrontational manner, the chances of him or her listening to you and understanding your concern is much greater. However, if you come across as accusatory and demeaning, it will often lead to a battle of the wills and neither of you win. Keep in mind that your main objective here is to influence and change a potentially harmful behavior or attitude, and the best way to do that is with genuine and honest dialogue.

Compromise doesn't always mean that you are accepting, or rejecting, personality traits and habits. Oftentimes compromise simply means giving up something you want as an individual for something that benefits you as a couple. An example of this may be money or time that you want to devote to a particular hobby or activity that you enjoy, but that also prohibits you as a married couple from doing something that is necessary for your well-being or livelihood. Perhaps you want to invest in a hobby that takes up a higher percentage of the household income that could be otherwise used to pay bills, reduce debt, or purchase some much-needed household improvements.

When you choose to delay a personal purchase—or perhaps you choose not to invest time in a sport or hobby so you can spend time together as a couple building your relationship—you are investing in your marriage and practicing the art of compromise. Compromise is putting the needs of your relationship before your individual needs. When you both do this, your marriage enjoys the very best that you can offer and the quality of your time grows exponentially. When your relationship is put before individual needs, you both win.

Compromise doesn't mean sacrificing your wants, needs, and desires of your relationship either. Compromise is a two-way street; and when both of you honor and respect one another, you will find that more often than not the end result is a closer and more satisfying relationship. You may even see that as you compromise more and more for your spouse, they, in turn, will do the same for you and the wants and needs that you both have will begin to be met time and time again.

Honesty

"Freedom from deceit or fraud; honorable in principles, intentions, and actions."[7]

Honesty is a very important piece to the puzzle in achieving the successful and excellent marriage you are seeking. When there is a firm foundation of honesty between one other, there are incredible freedoms that are experienced in the marriage, on both sides. Both spouses should feel confident in the marriage and come to expect honesty with regards to anything that may challenge the marriage. When you develop a pattern of trust, the level of honesty that you can expect from one another gives you the freedom to express your fears, your dreams, and the desires of your heart, without being fearful of what your spouse may say or think.

At times, you may feel that something that transpired during the course of your day isn't really that important, and you may choose not to share it with your spouse, but we encourage you to share everything with one another, and to hold no secrets. What may seem insignificant to you may mean a great deal to your spouse.

Recently Debby was at one of her coffee meetings with a friend of hers and as she was ordering her coffee, the barista was a bit overly friendly as he appeared to be trying to flirt with her. As she was telling me the account of what had happened, I thought to myself how easy it would be for me to feel thoughts of jealousy or even anger. In a relationship that is less stable, the husband may even think that his wife was encouraging this type of behavior and was reciprocating the flirting. It is important to remember that we cannot be responsible for the actions of others. If someone flirts with Debby, I have absolute confidence in her and in our relationship so I don't need to worry about it—that goes for the coffee barista and anyone else.

---

7 http://dictionary.reference.com/browse/honesty

Debby has the freedom to relate that incident to me, not being fearful of how I may respond. I didn't jump in my car to go down to the local coffee shop to exact my revenge on the barista or report him to corporate for inappropriate behavior. No, I actually had a moment of pride that my bride is beautiful enough to elicit the attention of others. By sharing that experience with me, it also reinforces my trust in Debby that she will be honest with me in all things.

Respect

"To hold in esteem or honor, to show regard or consideration for"[8]

Earlier in chapter 1 we talked about choosing to love your spouse, every morning and in a manner that far exceeds their expectations. We believe that the word "respect" and the verb definition of it go hand in hand when related to marriage. If you choose to honor your spouse and hold them in high esteem, and you do it in a very practical way every day, then your spouse will flourish and thrive knowing they are greatly valued, honored, and respected. You will build their esteem and self-confidence. When your spouse is elevated to a place of honor and respect, he or she will be more likely to invest in your relationship as well. As with most things in your relationship, it is reciprocal.

When you meet the needs of your spouse above your own, your spouse will begin to mirror your attitude and actions and begin to do the same for you. When there is mutual respect and each spouse holds the other in high esteem, in tangible and visible ways, you will begin to see your marriage move from mediocre to amazing. It will not happen overnight, nor will it happen over a short period of time. However, if both of you are consistent and invest in each other everyday, after a period of time your marriage will be elevated to the next level. You and your spouse may notice it at different times and the changes may be subtle at first, but your marriage will continue to reach new heights.

Before you know it, people will begin to ask you and your spouse what it is that you have in your marriage that is different, and how can they get it, too. They will ask you how it is possible that you can be so in love and treat one another as newlyweds when you have been married

---

8 http://dictionary.reference.com/browse/respect

for years. Others will be attracted to the joy and the love that you share, and they will recognize that your relationship is unique. We believe respect for each other is crucially important.

Biblical Perspective

God's Word is full of guidelines for holy living and relationships. Rather than break down each of the above individual categories, we will sum them all up in this one segment. Perhaps Colossians 3:1–15 covers the majority of these elements. It reads,

> "Since you have been raised to new life with Christ, set your sights on the realities of heaven, where Christ sits in the place of honor at God's right hand. Think about the things of heaven, not the things of earth. For you died to this life, and your real life is hidden with Christ in God. And when Christ, who is your life, is revealed to the whole world, you will share in all his glory. So put to death the sinful, earthly things lurking within you. Have nothing to do with sexual immorality, impurity, lust, and evil desires. Don't be greedy, for a greedy person is an idolater, worshiping the things of this world. Because of these sins, the anger of God is coming. You used to do these things when your life was still part of this world. But now is the time to get rid of anger, rage, malicious behavior, slander, and dirty language. Don't lie to each other, for you have stripped off your old sinful nature and all its wicked deeds. Put on your new nature, and be renewed as you learn to know your Creator and become like him. In this new life, it doesn't matter if you are a Jew or a Gentile, circumcised or uncircumcised, barbaric, uncivilized, slave, or free. Christ is all that matters, and he lives in all of us. Since God chose you to be the holy people he loves, you must clothe yourselves with tenderhearted mercy, kindness, humility, gentleness, and patience. Make allowance for each other's faults, and forgive anyone who offends you. Remember, the Lord forgave you, so you must forgive others. Above all, clothe yourselves with love, which binds us all together in perfect harmony. And let the peace that comes from Christ rule in your hearts. For as members of one body you are called to live in peace. And always be thankful."

Colossians 3:2 tells us to think about the things of heaven, or, in other words, set our minds on things above. (NIV) Philippians 4:8 says, "And now, dear brothers and sisters, one final thing. Fix your thoughts on what is true, and honorable, and right, and pure, and lovely, and admirable. Think about things that are excellent and worthy of praise." When you think about things that are excellent and worthy of praise, you have a mindset that is similar to what Christ had, and you will invest your time and efforts in other people. Specifically, you should invest in your spouse and in your marriage.

As followers of Christ, we are sanctified, which means that we are set apart from the world by the Spirit. We are called to be different; we should not live like the world lives, act like the world acts, or even look like the world. Christ wants us to be different from the world, so others will know there is a difference and seek the truth. Jesus gave of Himself when he was here on earth, and we are to give of ourselves to our spouse. We always need to be aware of the things that our spouse wants or needs and be willing to fulfill their needs with consistency. This is part of the art of compromise.

"Love is patient and kind. Love is not jealous or boastful or proud or rude. It does not demand its own way. It is not irritable, and it keeps no record of being wronged. It does not rejoice about injustice but rejoices whenever the truth wins out. Love never gives up, never loses faith, is always hopeful, and endures through every circumstance." 1 Corinthians 13:4–7.

Chapter 12

Resolving Conflict

"The quality of our lives depends not on whether or not we have conflicts, but on how we respond to them." ~ Tom Crum

Have you ever seen the commercial that asks, "Got milk?" Of course, many variations of that popular slogan have hit the airwaves, billboards, bumper stickers, and T-shirts. If we were to ask, "Got conflict?" every one of us at some point in our lives would have to respond with a resounding, "Yes." Conflicts occur in amazing marriages, just as they occur in disastrous marriages and every marriage in between. The question is not do you have conflict, but the question is how do you respond to the conflict that is sure to come?

I often say that anytime you have two or more people involved in anything—a project, a task, goal, or relationship—conflict is inevitable. People have differing viewpoints, ideas, preferences, habits, historical perspective, and even beliefs, and these all have the potential for igniting conflicting opinions. Conflict isn't all bad, as sometimes conflict causes us to examine a decision or action and oftentimes a better or more efficient solution is the net result of the conflict. If handled correctly, conflict can be good for your relationship. Additionally, conflict isn't always contentious and problematic; it depends on how you approach resolution.

We all have differing viewpoints on certain matters. No one else thinks like you do, so there is bound to be occasion where your viewpoint is in conflict with that of your spouse. It doesn't mean that one of you is right and the other wrong, sometimes it's just a healthy difference. Discussing your differing viewpoints may add options that you have never considered.

There will be times when your ideas or preferences are in conflict with your spouse. Again, it doesn't mean that your ideas are better or worse than his or hers, they are just different and they need to be discussed and weighed, and then a decision must be made as to which

161

route or choice to make. One preference difference that we continually address is the comfort level of the house. Debby is perennially cold and prefers the heat to be turned up all the time. It could be, and actually is at this very moment, seventy degrees in our house and she is wearing a long-sleeve undershirt along with a turtleneck or a sweatshirt. I am usually turning the heat down or opening a window, which sometimes leads to a low-level conflict. In recent years, I have learned to let this go and just wear lightweight shirts around the house.

One thing that we have personally learned very quickly is to keep what we call "short accounts." If we have a disagreement with one another, or with someone else, we try and resolve it as soon as possible. This is one of the key components in our marriage. No marriage or relationship can flourish and blossom if there is unresolved conflict that has not been dealt with. The longer it takes to work out your differences, the more difficult it could potentially be to find resolution that satisfies all parties.

> Unresloved conflict can escalate minor disagreements into major problems.

You aren't guaranteed tomorrow. None of us know for certain whether or not we will see another sunrise or sunset. You don't know if you will have an opportunity to resolve your differences with someone if you wait. How tragic it would be to have unresolved conflict with your best friend and lover if or when a tragic accident snatches him or her away from you. I think the emotions and pain associated with the loss of your lover would be magnified if there was unresolved anger or frustration, which would never be resolved. I, for one, would not want to live with the guilt that I would endure. To have unresolved conflict that continues for days, weeks, months, or even years on end is to take a risk that you may never resolve your differences. Keeping your accounts short and dealing with conflict in a timely manner will help to minimize that risk.

Unresolved conflict

Unresolved conflict may be one of the biggest threats to your marriage. Conflict, when left without resolution, has a way of growing and evolving into something potentially more damaging the longer it is ignored. When conflict is allowed to continue without resolution, the anger that you feel begins to take on a life of its own and tends to escalate in importance and intensity. Unresolved conflict has the potential to lead to additional problems and can escalate minor disagreements into major problems.

One of the choices we have made in our relationship is to never go to bed angry or with unresolved issues. Let me tell you from experience, this has not been an easy choice for us. There are times when we have a conflict of some sort and the last thing we want to do is come together to discuss it. Or discuss anything for that matter. Keep in mind that an amazing marriage is not without conflict and is certainly not without disagreements. You may have plenty of things pop up in your amazing marriage that you are not in complete agreement over initially, but the fact that you care enough about each other to resolve these differences is part of what some refer to as the magic of your relationship. It is not wrong or uncommon to have disagreements, but we have done our best to avoid allowing these disagreements to carry over into the following day.

Because of this choice to deal with conflict immediately, we have endured a number of late-night conversations (okay, arguments and fights) through the years that seemed to never end before 2:00 AM. Regardless of how intense they were, we have always thought it to be important for us to deal with today's problems today. If instead we choose to deal with yesterday's or last week's problems today, we may never find the time to deal with the new challenges that each day brings. It's like doing yesterday's work today on your job; you may not have time to catch up and accomplish today's work. As much as possible, begin and end each day with a clean slate.

Historically, our most intense discussions or arguments take place long after the kids are settled in their beds and the house is quiet. This seems to be the case because with our work schedule and the activities of our kids, we typically can't focus on ourselves until after they are in bed. With our commitment to not go to bed angry, we sometimes find ourselves dealing with problems late into the night. Now, this doesn't always mean that the conflict is completely resolved before we go to sleep. Some problems are much greater than that and take considerably more time to resolve. If it is a long and complicated issue, sometimes we agree to table the discussion until the following day, but we do so without anger or bitterness. We are usually successful at resolution the following day once we get past the anger and decide to set aside time to talk.

Another little tidbit of advice is this: do not sleep apart due to conflict or anger. We think you should never sleep separately, but we do realize that under certain circumstances it cannot be avoided. However, once you set a precedent of sleeping apart due to a fight or unresolved conflict, it will become easier and easier to repeat this choice and it will most definitely affect your marriage. You may begin to drift apart and avoid conflict or difficult discussions altogether. Sleeping apart has the potential to begin a habit or routine that should be avoided at all cost. It seems so easy for one spouse to sleep on the couch during a fight, but we think that it may also become too easy to continue that practice. Once the decision has been made to sleep apart, for whatever reason, the habit is extremely difficult to break later. In over twenty years of marriage, we have never slept on the couch or in the other room to avoid or put off a fight until the following morning. If you have done this in your marriage, we implore you to cease that practice and work through your current issues, at least to the point where you can resolve your anger and have a productive discussion the following day.

When we lived in New Mexico, we seemed to have a higher frequency of these late-night endeavors, and they usually preceded an important meeting or event I had at work the next day. As I reflect on that, I think it may be due to additional stress I was feeling from work that I brought home with me. Regardless of the cause, when we had a late-night argument, it seemed that more often than not I needed to wake up earlier than usual the next morning. I clearly recall several of these nights when I was desperate to just end the conversation and carry it on the following morning, but we knew our relationship was far more important than whatever meeting or event I had going on. Sleep would just have to wait.

There were many nights, while we were still learning how to communicate, that we would be up until the wee hours of the morning trying to work through an issue or disagreement. There were numerous occasions where Debby would lock herself in the bathroom and cry, not knowing what else to do and embarrassed to cry in front of me. It was during those times that I would always resolve to change the way I communicated, but three months later we would be right back where we started again. I only wish someone had intervened in our lives earlier so we could have avoided some of those fights and sleepless nights.

If you go to bed angry without resolving the issue at hand, it will be easier to do the same the next time you have an argument. If this continues, over time you may tend to put off conflict resolution and it will get easier and easier to ignore the problems. If you do that, the problem will not only still be there the next day, it will most likely take on a whole new dimension and you could have additional problems to deal with. Conflict needs to be taken care of and resolved as quickly and efficiently as possible.

Admittedly, I can have a pretty hot temper and it doesn't take too much to get me fired up. If this sounds like you, it is important for you to recognize that in yourself and find ways to control your anger. As I grow older, I am much more aware of circumstances that cause me to lose my temper. While I still struggle with this from time to time, I can typically walk away from a situation and cool off so long as I can recognize it coming. I have yet to figure out how to calm my short temper while driving, though!

If your emotions run hot during disagreements and conflicts and you find yourself responding with violence, such as yelling, name-calling, throwing things, and or causing property damage, you need to learn to control your temper and find a better way to vent your anger. For me, walking away and allowing myself some time to control my emotions has been an important part in conflict resolution.

I have never hit or physically injured Debby, but I can recall a number of things I have thrown against walls or the floor; something I am not proud of. A dish, a glass, or even the iron has all been an instrument of my wrath. I think the funniest moment, though it wasn't funny at the time, is when we started arguing over a game of Monopoly and Debby picked up the entire game board and threw it at me. I was peppered with houses, hotels, game pieces, paper money, and even the game board itself. To this very day, we have not played a game of Monopoly since that fateful night over fifteen years ago!

Resolving Conflict

There are several things that you can do with conflict, and how you handle conflict will have a direct impact on your relationship. You can choose to ignore it, blame one another for it, add to it, or address and resolve it. One thing is certain: conflict must be resolved to restore your fellowship and relationship. One thought that will pave the way for productive conflict resolution is to understand that the conflict is a challenge you both need to work through together, not a battle that must be won. Debby will address conflict resolution now.

As we mentioned earlier, we learned in our counseling that sometimes Jason just needs to hold me. This has been a wonderful tool that is extremely useful in resolving conflict. We learned that when we were in the heat of the battle and I was fighting to the death on a particular issue, Jason was to simply hold me. It was difficult at first, I will admit. In the middle of a fight when I was the angriest, the last thing I wanted Jason to do was to hold me, but that was really the most effective thing he could do. It shows me that no matter what the conflict, the anger, the words, or the attitude, we will make it through and resolve the conflict. It reminds me that he loves me and will continue to love me. It is his way of assuring me that we are going to be okay.

As you discuss an issue and resolve conflicts with your spouse, it is important to use phrases such as "I feel" rather than, "You make me feel." This demonstrates that you are taking responsibility for the way you feel, rather than putting blame on your spouse for causing you to feel the way you do. This small shift may change the attitude of your spouse and have a positive impact on the resolution of the conflict.

My attitude usually changes after he holds me for a period of time. I settle down and realize that there is no issue we could face that is worth sacrificing our marriage over and that resolution and compromise are the best choices we can make. Now that I've said my piece on this, I'll let Jason take it again from here.

Discipline

We have found, particularly as our children are getting older, that we are not always initially in agreement when it comes to discipline. When our kids were much younger, we had previously established consequences for disobedience, and, as a couple, we didn't struggle with determining the appropriate discipline. I'm not sure if it is because their behavior was more predictable and repetitive when they were younger, but as our girls entered high school it became increasingly difficult for us to deal with their discipline and for Debby and me to be in complete agreement with one another as to the severity of the punishment.

In our family, like most families, one parent is typically stricter than the other and tends to administer discipline more forcefully than the other. We are not talking about physical force or abuse, but a tendency to set tougher punishments. One parent may have an idea of discipline that includes a harsher or longer penalty. Examples may include a longer time of restriction, a broader definition of what the restriction includes, additional chores, loss of the cell phone or computer privileges, etc. It is important for the two of you to talk these differences out together before you approach the child with the verdict.

As a married couple, if you cannot agree on a form or severity of punishment when your kids are disobedient, that disagreement can cause significant problems you need to deal with, in addition to the discipline problem with the child you are needing to address. You may find that you are arguing with your spouse over discipline and it may actually divert your attention away from the wayward child, where it should be.

There have been numerous times when one of our children has disobeyed and we delayed the punishment until we, as the parents, were in agreement. We didn't ignore the problem and fail to address it with the offending child; rather, we discussed the behavior to ensure he or she had a clear understanding of what they did wrong and what choice they should have made. Depending on the severity of the disobedience, we sometimes established an interim punishment and then discussed the options in greater detail between just the two of us. This approach allowed us the time to be unified in our decision making while still addressing the behavior in a timely manner.

We believe that it is important to never discipline a child while we are angry, so sometimes delaying the punishment allows us a cooling off period and also allows our child time to think about their poor choices. Punishing a child in the heat of the moment, when anger and disappointment are at their peak, may not always produce the best results. Therefore, communicating an interim set of restrictions or punishment gives us time to discuss the options and develop what we feel will be an appropriate response. There are some situations in which this does not apply and there are some situations in which we don't need to consider the options, but we would rather delay the consequences to ensure we are in complete agreement than for one of us to make a rash decision that may be either too punitive or inconsequential.

Above all else, when we need to discipline a child we believe it is very important that both of us are in agreement. If both parents are not in agreement with the discipline, it may be evident to the child and he or she may use that information to their advantage. The child may try to drive a wedge between us as parents by manipulating the situation and pitting us against one another. The child may find sympathy from the parent who does not agree with the punishment and may take advantage of that. A surefire way to cause conflict in your marriage is to allow your children to come in between the two of you.

Biblical Perspective

The Bible says in Ephesians 4:26, "And don't sin by letting anger control you. Don't let the sun go down while you are still angry." Anger, or conflict, can have a devastating effect on your relationship. It causes us to be critical of one another and it is divisive. Additionally, anger often leads to an escalation of the current issue at hand. Proverbs 29:11 says, "A fool gives full vent to his anger, but a wise man keeps himself under control." (NIV) Stick to the issue at hand and resolve your differences as quickly as possible, without using this as an opportunity to vent all your anger and add to the existing conflict. As often as possible, resolve your conflict before the sun goes down on your anger.

God's Word has plenty to say about keeping our communication positive and uplifting. Proverbs 15:1 instructs us to avoid words that stir up anger, "A gentle answer deflects anger, but harsh words make tempers flare." When we have arguments or disagreements, we are to avoid saying anything that will add fuel to the fire of disagreement. Proverbs 13: 3 says, "He who guards his lips guards his life, but he who speaks rashly will come to ruin." (NIV) We find in Proverbs 15: 4, "Gentle words are a tree of life, a deceitful tongue crushes the spirit."

When Debby and I have disagreements with one another and we heed the words of James 1:19 which says, "Understand this my dear brothers and sisters: You must all be quick to listen, slow to speak and slow to get angry," we typically find resolution and compromise that we can both agree to and we are able to avoid conflict. Listening to one another without interrupting or becoming argumentative will lead to a smoother resolution. Proverbs 18:13 says it this way, "He who answers before listening—that is his folly and his shame." (NIV)

We are committed to have a mutual respect for one another and we allow the other to openly share their feelings. In doing so, we validate the feelings we each have and we honor each other's point of view without ridicule. Proverbs 12:18 says, "Reckless words pierce like a sword, but the tongue of the wise brings healing." (NIV)

When forgiveness is needed, we forgive one another quickly and completely, without any strings attached or conditions. Forgiveness is critical to restoring the relationship, even if the disagreement or conflict seems small and insignificant. Unresolved conflict tends to lie dormant, ready to spring forth and attack when we least expect it. Forgiveness should be readily given and should not be limited. Luke 17:3–4 says, "If your brother sins, rebuke him, and if he repents, forgive him. If he sins against you seven times in a day, and seven times comes back to you and says, 'I repent,' forgive him." (NIV) Ephesians 4:32 says, "Instead, be kind to each other, tenderhearted, forgiving one another, just as God through Christ has forgiven you."

As you can see, God clearly desires us to resolve all conflict and disagreements with others immediately and completely. When we harbor unresolved conflict, our effectiveness is limited; refusing to forgive one another or work through conflict is sin, and God cannot and will not bless if we are living in sin. Ephesians 4:3 says, "Make every effort to keep yourselves united in the Spirit, binding yourselves together with peace."

> ...forgive one another quickly and completely.

Rick Warren said, "In fact, the tunnel of conflict is the passageway to intimacy in any relationship. Until you care enough to confront and resolve the underlying barriers, you will never grow close to each other."[1] When we harbor unresolved conflict, sex and intimacy are the farthest things from our minds. I must admit that even I, the one who always seems ready for intimacy, find it hard to desire to share intimacy when we are living with unresolved conflict. When we are harboring unresolved conflict, the air is heavy, almost like a fog, and nothing seems to be right. When we resolve the conflict and are restored in our fellowship, it is as if the fog burns away and the sun shines brightly. All is well again, and we resume our intimacy.

When conflict comes your way, consider it an opportunity for growth. When we successfully resolve conflict, our communication and problem-solving skills are tested. James 1:2–4 says, "Dear brothers and sisters, when troubles come your way, consider it an opportunity for great

---

1 Rick Warren, *The Purpose Driven Life: What on Earth Am I Here For?* (Michigan: Zondervan, 2007), 147

joy. For you know that when your faith is tested, your endurance has a chance to grow. So let it grow, for when your endurance is fully developed, you will be perfect and complete, needing nothing." Resolving conflict builds us up in our faith in God and builds us up in the eyes of our spouse. We are able to demonstrate both obedience to Christ and a commitment to our spouse. When we resolve conflict successfully, we build one another up and add value to one another, as we are instructed to do in 1 Thessalonians 5:11, "So encourage each other and build each other up, just as you are already doing."

Finally, we are instructed by God to resolve conflict. He doesn't want us living a defeated and limited life, which is exactly what Satan desires. With this in mind, strive to heed the words of Romans 12:17–21: "Never pay back evil with more evil. Do things in such a way that everyone can see you are honorable. Do all that you can to live in peace with everyone. Dear friends, never take revenge. Leave that to the righteous anger of God. For the Scriptures say, 'I will take revenge; I will pay them back,' says the Lord. Instead, 'If your enemies are hungry, feed them. If they are thirsty, give them something to drink. In doing this, you will heap burning coals of shame on their heads.' Don't let evil conquer you, but conquer evil by doing good."

Chapter 13

Discovering Your Amazing Marriage

"Success is the sum of small efforts, repeated day in and day out."
~ Robert J. Collier

By now, you should have a pretty good idea forming in your head of how you would rate your marriage in its current state, as well as some areas that you desire change or growth to occur. We have taken you through a self-evaluation process and we have given you several ideas you can initiate that will elevate your marriage and add value to your spouse. Perhaps the only question left in your mind is where and how to begin.

The first step in discovering the amazing marriage that you and your spouse are capable of achieving occurs in your mind. You must choose to make your marriage amazing. You must choose to value your spouse and make him or her feel as if they are the most important person in the entire world to you, and you must choose to remind them of that very fact on a daily basis. You must also choose that the one you married is the one to whom you pledge your eternal love and commitment, no matter the cost.

Whether your marriage is strong and growing on a continual basis or if you are one crisis away from a disastrous divorce, you have the ability to influence your marriage. We have walked you through some steps that will impact your life in the most powerful and amazing way, if you choose to love your spouse in a completely selfless manner. No matter where you are in your marriage today, one thing is certain: the choices you make regarding your spouse and your marriage will have an impact with immediate and long-lasting results.

If you have not yet begun to make some changes in your daily activities or in the choices you make, recommit yourself today to your husband or your wife and make today the first day in your quest to discover your amazing marriage. Make the conscious decision today that your

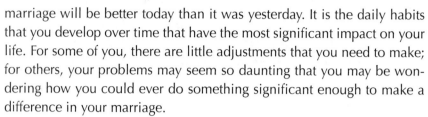

marriage will be better today than it was yesterday. It is the daily habits that you develop over time that have the most significant impact on your life. For some of you, there are little adjustments that you need to make; for others, your problems may seem so daunting that you may be wondering how you could ever do something significant enough to make a difference in your marriage.

The most important decision you need to make is the decision that you need to do something. If you have previously settled for mediocrity in your marriage and now you realize that you want more, you need to decide to do something about it. Change won't happen automatically and improvements won't occur simply because you want them to happen. You must decide that you will initiate some change in your attitude or actions, and you need to step out in faith. The biggest and oftentimes the most fearful step you will take in improving your marriage is the very first step. Take that step today and decide that you will choose to do whatever it takes to make your marriage amazing.

Before you pillow your head tonight, make sure you tell your spouse, at least once, that you love him or her. When you say the words "I LOVE YOU," say them with meaning, with passion, with fervor, and with zeal. At some point throughout your day, express your love to your spouse in a meaningful way. If you are not in the habit of expressing your love on a daily basis to your spouse, let us encourage you to make this a daily habit—not a habit that is merely a routine or something arduous that you have to do, but a habit that makes a profound statement. If necessary, leave a reminder for yourself that you will see each day to prompt you to demonstrate this love to your spouse.

Throughout the process of writing this book, we have wrestled with how much detail we would include as far as our personal struggles and failures. We all have skeletons in our closets and we've all suffered loss and failure. Debby and I have decided that it would be easier for you, our readers, to make a personal application if you were able to get a glimpse of some of our personal struggles. Our sincere desire is that through our examples and words of encouragement, you will discover the kind of amazing marriage that we have developed. Perhaps you will be able to avoid some of the failures we have experienced as you learn to apply the principles found in these pages to your own relationship.

We recognize that our marriage requires effort on a daily basis. Some days are full of joy and success, and other days we struggle. But even through our struggles we are victorious. We realize we have more growth yet to come, and we are continuing our habits of putting one another first and adding value to each other. As we do this, we continue to discover ways to value one another and the result is a deeper relationship.

We trust you will continue to grow closer together and you will strengthen your relationship on a daily basis. Marriage can be amazing, and we trust and pray that you will discover this to be true of your relationship as well. May God truly bless you and your marriage. For more encouragement for your marriage or for information on how you can have a personal relationship with God, visit www.youramazingmarriage.com.

Meet the Authors

Debby was raised in western Washington. Prior to having children, she worked as a legal secretary. Debby quit her job several months after the birth of their first daughter and was a stay-at-home mom for fourteen years. For the past four years, she has worked as a part-time substitute secretary for our local school district.

Jason was born in Louisville, Kentucky, and raised in Arizona, moving to Washington while a sophomore in high school. He was raised by his mother, with his brother and two sisters. Jason went to work on a part-time basis for a sporting goods company when he was nineteen years old and has worked his way up the corporate ladder, where he is currently a District Supervisor in the greater Seattle-Tacoma vicinity. He has twenty-three years of retail sporting goods experience, nineteen of which have been in various leadership roles.

Jason and Debby have both been active in the local church for the majority of their marriage, working in various ministries with their main focus working with teens and children. They have been active leaders in the Awana ministry for nineteen years as well as serving on the Awana Ministry Team for the Pacific Northwest. Jason has also served as an elder-elect and he has coordinated the Outreach Ministry in a local church. They have a heart for missions and have been on several mission trips to Rio de Janeiro, Brasil.

Jason and Debby have four children, three daughters and a son, ranging in age from eighteen to eleven. They are extremely involved in the lives of their children, as the kids are active in sports, school activities, church youth groups, and much more.

Jason and Debby Coleman celebrated their twentieth wedding anniversary in September of 2009, and they currently live in Federal Way, Washington.

① Summer Hymn
   assist Carmela

② Zip Line - rebuild

③ will & Sarah - CA

④ Tom - Last wife

⑤ John -

⑥ austin

Praise

①